Table of Contents

THE HABIT

STOP GETTING IN YOUR OWN WAY

It's Time To Rid Yourself Of The Bad Habits Holding You Back From Abundant Success

Lewis Delgado

Chapter 1:

How to Determine What Makes You Happy

Finding your happiness is an art, not science, but here are five things I've done to help me figure where my happiness is coming from.

1. Wipe Your Happiness Slate Clean

If you're a human who is alive, the society you grew up in has Ideas about what happiness looks like. These ideas have permeated our lives since the moment we could understand shapes and colors; they've wormed their way into our soft, sweet subconsciouses.

On some level, most of us believe we will be happier when:

- We are thinner than we are now

- We earn more money

- We live in a bigger, prettier, better-located home

- We have more friends

- We're in a committed romantic relationship

And maybe some of those things really will make us happier! Supportive relationships and aerobic activity have been shown to reduce depression.

I imagine moving into a space with more natural light, and a shorter commute wouldn't hurt anything, either.

But for the sake of this experiment, let's do our very, very best to let go of preconceived notions about what makes us happy. Let's forget what our families and friends believe happiness looks like. Let's view this as a grand experiment with totally unknown results. Who knows what we'll discover!

P.S. Don't get down on yourself for "buying into cultural expectations of happiness." We all do it. We're not robots. For Pete's sake, Oprah's been trying to diet her way to happiness for two decades.

2. Start Taking Detailed Notes When You Feel Really Happy

Do you know those moments of "_If this isn't nice, I don't know what is_"? Those moments when you'd lift your face to the sky and grin (but you don't because it feels awkward), make a note of _those_ moments. Open up the 'notes' app on your phone and type in what, exactly, you were doing.

Yes, I know this is dorky. And, yes, I know you're thinking, "I should do that!" And then you're not going to do it.
_Do it._ I think you'll be surprised by what makes you happy.

3. Remind yourself, "This makes me happy."

Many of the things that make me happy are, to be honest, a hassle (and by 'hassle,' I mean "require me to put on real clothes, google something, and leave the house"). Intellectually, I know taking a day trip to Hudson, working in a new coffee shop, and then hanging out on the sandbar will make me happy … but it is just SO MUCH EASIER to keep working at home in my yoga pants.

Here's how I remember what makes me happy:

- I wrote a list of the things that make me happy – big and little, easy and difficult – and posted that list next to my computer. Whenever my mind wanders, whenever I'm feeling blue, I can look to the right of my computer screen and remember that reading a chapter of <u>this</u> book while cuddling the dog will make me happy.

- When I'm in the middle of doing something that makes me happy, I say to myself, "This makes me happy."

Am I eating chocolate mousse at a supper club in rural South Dakota? *"This makes me happy."*

Am I hiking around a lake on a sunny Tuesday afternoon? *"This makes me happy."*

I just bought an amazing chair on Craigslist for $50? *"This makes me happy."*

Reciting this little phrase helps cement these happy-making habits in my brain and life. It helps me feel proud to take steps to have the life I want. It reminds me that the hassle of happiness – the planning, the boundary-pushing, the saving, and scheduling – is worth it.

Chapter 2:

Six Habits of Self-Love

We can show gratitude to ourselves for our different achievements in many ways. It is something that most people overlook as a waste of time and resources. This is a fallacy. It is high time we develop habits of self-love, to recharge our bodies and minds in preparation for another phase of achievements.

Here are six habits of self-love:

1. Treating Yourself

It is showing gratitude to yourself by way of satisfying your deepest desires instead of waiting for someone else to do it for you. Take the personal initiative to go shopping and buy that designer suit or dress you have been wanting so badly. Do not wait for someone else to do it for you while you are capable.

Take that much-needed vacation and a break from work to be with your family. Spend time with the people you love and cherish every moment because, in this fast-moving world, the future is uncertain. Secure your happiness lest you drown in depression. The best person to take care of your interests is yourself.

Who will take you out for swimming or outing to those posh hotels if you do not initiate it? Self-love begins when you realize your worth and do not allow anyone else to bring it down.

2. Celebrate Your Victories

Take advantage of every opportunity to celebrate your wins, no matter how small. A habit of self-love is to celebrate your achievements and ignore voices that discourage you. Nothing should muffle you from shouting your victories to the world. The testimony of your victory will encourage a stranger not to give up in his/her quest.

It is neither pride nor boastfulness. It is congratulating yourself for the wins that you rightfully deserve. How else can you love yourself if you do not appreciate yourself for the milestones you have conquered? Do not shy away from thanking yourself, privately or publicly, because no one else best knows your struggles except yourself.

3. Accept Yourself

To begin with, accept your social and economic status because you know the battles you have fought. Self-acceptance is an underrated form of self-love. Love yourself and accept your shortcomings. When you learn to accept yourself, other people will in turn accept you. They will learn how to accommodate you in the same manner you learned to live with all your imperfections.

Self-loathing dies when you master self-acceptance and self-love. Self-care keeps off self-rejection. You begin seeing your worth and great potential. It is the enemy within that is responsible for the fall of great empires.

The enemy within is low self-esteem and self-rejection. Accept the things you cannot change and change the things in your ability. Do not be hard on yourself because a journey of a thousand miles begins with a single step.

4. Practice Forgiveness

Forgiveness is a strong act. When you forgive those who wrong you, you let go of unnecessary baggage. It is unhealthy to live with a heart full of hate (pun intended). Forgiveness does not mean that you have allowed other people to wrong you repetitively. It means you have outgrown their wrong acts and you no longer allow their inconsiderate acts to affect you. Forgiveness benefits the forgiver more than the forgiven. It heals the heart from any hurt caused. It is the best form of self-care yet difficult at the same time. Forgiveness is a gradual process initiated by the bigger person in any conflict. Practicing self-care is by recognizing the importance of turning a new leaf and staying free from shackles of grudges and bitterness.

Unforgiveness builds bitterness and vengeance. It finally clouds your judgment and you become irrational. Choosing forgiveness is a vote on self-care.

5. Choose Your Associates Wisely

Associate with progressive people. Show me your friends and I will tell you the kind of person you are. Your friends have the potential to either build or destroy your appreciation of self-worth. They will trim your excesses and supplement your deficiencies. A cadre of professionals tends to share several traits.

Self-care involves taking care of your mental state and being selective of who you let into your personal space. It supersedes all other interests.

6. Engaging In Hobbies

Hobbies are the activities we do during our free time to relax our minds and bond with our friends. When doing these hobbies we are at ease and free from pressures of whatever form. We need to take a break from our daily work routine from time to time and do other social activities.

Hobbies are essential to explore other interests and rejuvenate our psyche and morale. Self-love places your interests and well-being above everything else. There is a thin line between it and selfishness, but it is not the latter.

These six habits of self-love will ensure you have peace and sobriety of mind to make progressive decisions.

Chapter 3:

How To Use Affirmations For Success

Affirmations are best described as a self-help strategy that is used to promote self-confidence and belief in your abilities. There might come a million instances where you felt like you needed to affirm yourself, and there would be many moments when you have probably affirmed yourself without even realizing it. Simple sentences like "I've got what it takes" or "I believe in my ability to succeed" shift your focus away from the perceived inadequacies or failures and direct your focus towards your strengths. While affirmations may not be a magic bullet for instant success, they generally work as a tool for shifting your mindset and achieving your goals.

Neuroplasticity, or our brain's ability to adapt and change to different circumstances throughout our lives, makes us understand what makes affirmations work and how to make them more effective. Creating a mental image beforehand of doing something that you're scared of, like acing a nerve-wracking interview or bungee jumping to conquer your fear of heights, can encourage your brain to take these positive affirmations as fact, and soon your actions will tend to follow.

Repeating affirmations can help you boost your confidence and motivation, but you still must take some action yourself. Affirmations are a step towards the change, not the change itself. They can also help you to achieve your goals by strengthening your confidence by reminding you that you're in control of your success and what you can do right now to achieve it. Affirmations give you a list of long-standing patterns and beliefs, and it makes you act as if you've already succeeded. Understand that affirmations alone can't produce a change in every situation. You have to take some actions too along with them. Similarly, affirming your traits can also help you see yourself in a new light.

To get the most benefits from affirmations, start a regular practice and make it a habit. Say affirmations upon waking up and getting into bed; give them at least 3-5 minutes. Repeat each of your affirmations ten times, focus on the words that leave your mouth. Believe them to be true while saying them. Make it a consistent habit. You have to be patient and stick with your practice, and it might take some time before you see evident changes. Practicing affirmations can also activate the reward system in your brain, which can impact how you experience both emotional and physical pain. The moment you start managing your stress and other life difficulties, it would help you promote faith in yourself and boost self-empowerment.

Chapter 4:

<u>10 Habits of Happy People</u>

Happy people live the most satisfying lives on the planet. They have come to understand the importance of not worrying because it will not make any differential change in their lives. If you cannot control the outcome of a process, why worry? If you can control and make a difference to the outcome of a situation, why worry? Worrying does not bring an ounce of success your way.

Here are 10 habits of happy people that could be you if you choose to adopt it:

1. <u>Happy People Count Their Blessings.</u>

Taking stock of your successes is an important part of appreciating yourself. You find comfort in knowing that despite all the hiccups you have found in your journey there remains an oasis of achievements in your desert.

Everyone needs to take stock of what is in his or her basket of blessings. It is a reminder of your resilience and persistence in the face of challenges. It is an indication of your ability and a minute representation of the progress you can make, given time.

Remind yourself of the taste of victory in your small achievements. It begins with understanding that you definitely cannot be able to win it all. There are grey and shadow areas that will not be within your reach.

2. Happy People Do Not Need the Validation of Others.

Happy people do not wait for the validation of other people. They are autonomous. Develop the habit of doing what is right regardless of your audience and you will have an authentic lifestyle. As such, your source of happiness will be independent of uncontrollable factors. Why should you tie your happiness to someone else capable of ruining your day in a snap? This is not to mean that you will not need other people. Humans are social beings and interdependent. Letting them strongly influence your lifestyle is the major problem. Be your own man.

3. They Are Bold.

Boldly and cautiously pursuing their ambitions is part of the ingredients that make up happy people. Knowing what you want is one thing and pursuing it is another. If music is your passion and it makes you happy, chase after it for it is therein that your happiness lies. Whatever it is (of course considering its legality) do not let it pass.

To be truly happy, do not live in the shadow of other happy people. Define your happiness and drink from your well. Timidity will make you bask under the shade of giants and create a sense of false security. One day the shade will be no more and leave you exposed to an unimaginable reality.

4. They are social people.

Being social is one common characteristic of happy people. Happiness makes them bubbly and alive. There is a common testament in almost all happy people – either happiness made them social or their social nature made them happy. Thanks to whichever of the two came earlier, they are happy people!

Like bad luck, happiness is contagious. Your social circle can infect you with happiness or even deny it to you. Being sociable does not mean to the extreme nature with all the hype that comes along.

It means being approachable to people. Some will positively add to your basket and others will offer positive criticism towards your cause. With such input, your happiness will have longevity.

5. Believe in a greater cause.

Happy people understand that it is not always about them. There is a greater cause above their interests. They do not derive their happiness from the satisfaction of their needs and wants. Regardless of any deficiency in their lives, their flame of happiness is not easily put out.

Do you want to be happy? It is time to put self-interest aside and not tie your happiness to local anchors. An average person's happiness is mainly dependent on his well-being. Refusing to be average gives you leverage over those out to put off your happiness.

6. Lead a purposeful life.

Are there happy people without purpose? Those we see happy maintain their status by having a powerful drive towards the same. A strong purpose will make you stay on happiness' lane. It is the habit of happy people to have a purpose. This is to enable them to stay on course.

Being happy is not a permanent state. It is easily reversible if caution is not taken. Purposefulness is part of the caution taken by happy people.

7. Admit they are human.

To err is human. Given this, happy people appreciate the erroneous nature of man and accept the things they cannot change, have the courage to change the things they can, and the wisdom to know the difference. A prayer commonly referred to as the serenity prayer.

Admitting being human is the first step towards being happy. You forgive yourself of your wrongs before seeking the forgiveness of another. This brings inner peace culminating in happiness.

8. Know their strengths and weaknesses.

Being aware of your strengths and weaknesses is one thing happy people have mastered. Through that, they know their limits; the time to push and time to take a break. This serves to help avoid unwarranted disappointments that come along with new challenges.

Nothing can put off the charisma of a prepared spirit. Happy people know their limitations well enough such that no ill-willed voice can whisper disappointments to them. They hold the power of self-awareness within their hearts making them live with contentment.

9. Notice the contributions of those around them.

No man is an island. The contributions of other people in our lives cannot be emphasized enough. We are because they are (for all the good reasons). At any one point in our lives, someone made us happy. The first step is noticing the roles played by those in our immediate environment.

The joy of being surrounded by people to hold our hands in life is engraved deeper in our hearts in times of need. It is time you stop looking far away and turn your eyes to see what is next to you.

10. They are grateful and appreciative.

"Thank you" is a word that does not depart from the lips of happy people. Their hearts are trained to focus on what is at their disposal instead of what they cannot reach. It is crystal that a bird in hand is worth two in the bush.

Happy people continue being happy despite deficiencies. Try being appreciative and see how happiness will tow along.

Adopt these 10 habits of happy people and depression will keep away from you. If you want to be happy, do what happy people do and you will see the difference.

Chapter 5:

Your Motivational Partner In Life

We all have friends. We all have parents. We may have a partner or other half. We all have teachers.

We love and respect all of them and hopefully, they do too. But have we ever wondered why we do that?

Why do we have to love someone who brought us into this world? Why do we love a person who is not related to us whatsoever, but has a connection with us, and hence we like to hang around them? Why do we respect someone who is being paid to do what makes him respectable?

The answer to all these is simple. They make us a better version of ourselves. Without these people in our lives, we won't be as good as we are right now.

It doesn't matter where we stand right now in our lives, there would always be someone backing you up whenever you feel low.

People tend to seek loneliness and a quiet corner whenever life hits hard. But what they don't realize is that there are people in their lives who have a duty towards you.

Either that be your parents or friends or partner or anyone for that case, you need to find time to give them a chance to show their true affections towards you. You need to give them

Your parents can't give up on you because you are a part of them. You have their legacy to keep and spread. They want you to be a better person than they ever were, hence they will always support you no matter what the world does to you.

Your friends have a bond of loyalty towards you which is the basic root of any friendship. They will always try to help you get up no matter how many times you fall.

All these people owe you this support. And you owe it to them to be a source of inspiration when they want a shoulder to cry. When they want a person to listen and feel their pain. When they need someone to be able to share some time with them without a grain of self-interest.

These things make us stronger as a human and make us grow and evolve as a Specie.

You can find motivation and inspiration from anyone. It may even be a guard in your office or a worker in your office who you might see once a week.

Basic human nature makes us susceptible to the need of finding company. It doesn't matter where it comes from. What you need is a person who can devote a selfless minute of his or her life to you and feels good when they realize they have made a positive change in your life.

Everyone goes through this phase of loneliness but we always find a person who makes us the most comfortable.

The person who reimburses our self-belief. The person who makes us take one more try, one more chance, not for us but for them too. This person is your true motivational partner in life.

Chapter 6:

10 Habits That Can Ruin Your Day

Habits are the building blocks of our day. No matter how you spin it, either way, every detail matters.

The little actionable habits eventually sets you up to a either having a fulfilling day, or one that you have just totally wasted away. Nothing is as bad as destructive habits as they sabotage your daily productivity. Slowly, you slip further and further until it's too late when you've realized the damage that they have done to your life.

Bad habits are insidious! They drag down your life, lowers down your levels of accuracy, and make your performance less creative and stifling. It is essential, not only for productivity, to gain control of your bad habits. AS Grenville Kleiser once noted, "Constant self-discipline and self-control help you develop greatness of character." Nonetheless, it is important to stop and ask: what do you need today to get rid of or change? Sure, you can add or adjust new skills into your daily life.

Below are ten persistent habits that can ruin your day's success and productivity.

1. Hitting The Snooze Button.

Your mind, while you sleep, moves through a comprehensive series of cycles, the last one alerting you to wake up. While you crave for ten more minutes of sleep as the alarm goes off, what do you do? You whacked the snooze button. We're all guilty of this! If you don't suck it up, rip off the cover and start your morning, the rest of your day will be flawed. How do you expect your day to be strong once you don't start it off strong? You will feel far more optimistic, strong and fully prepared when you wake up without hitting the snooze button. So avoid the snooze button at any cost if you want a productive day ahead!

2. Wasting Your "Getting Ready" Hours.

You might need to reconsider the scrolling of Instagram and Facebook or the inane program you put on behind the scenes while preparing. These things have a time and place to partake in them – for example when you've accomplished your day's work and need some time to unwind and relax; however the time isn't now. Your morning schedule ought to be an interaction that prepares and energizes you for the day ahead. The objective is to accomplish something that animates your mind within the first hour of being conscious, so you can be more inventive, invigorated, gainful, and connected with all through the entire day! Avoiding this sweeps you away from normalizing the worst habit you might have: distraction. Instead, give yourself a chance to breathe the fine morning, anticipate the day's wonder and be thankful for whatever you have.

3. Failing To Prioritize Your Breakfast.

Energizing your day is essential if you wish for a very productive day. Energizing your body system requires that you prioritize eating your breakfast. However, the contents of your breakfast must entail something that will ensure that your day is not slowed down by noon. This means a blend of high - fiber foods such as proteins and healthy must be incorporated. Avoid taking too many sugars and heavy starches. The goal is to satiate and energize your body for the day.

4. Ruminating on the Problems of Yesterday And Negativity.

Don't take yesterday's problems to your new day if you want to start your day off right. If the day before you had difficult meetings and talks and you woke up ruminating about your horrific experiences, leave that negativity at your doorway. Moreover, if the problem you are lamenting about have been solved, then you shouldn't dwell on the past. Research suggests that we usually encounter more positive than negative events in a day. Still, often your mind concentrates on the negative due to a subconscious distortion called the negative distortion. By choosing not to focus on negative events and thinking about what's going well, you can learn to take advantage of the strength of the positive events around us. Raising negativity only increases stress. Let go of it and get on without it!

5. Leaving Your Day To Randomness.

Do not let stuff just simply happen to you; do it. Failure to create a structured day leads to a totally random day. A random day lacking direction, focus, and efficiency. Distractions will also creep into your day more readily because you have allowed randomness to happen to you. Instead, have a clear and precise list of what you need to focus for the day. This serves as a framework and a boundary for you to work within. Another thing you should consider is to spend your first 90 minutes on the most thoughtful and important task for the day. This allows you to know the big things out right at the beginning, reducing your cognitive burden for the rest of the day.

6. Becoming Involved With the Overview.

How frequently have you woken up, and before you can stretch and grin, you groan pretty much all the have-to for now and the fragmented musts from yesterday? This unhealthy habit will ruin your great day ahead. Know and understand these are simply contemplations. You can decide to recalibrate by pondering all you must be thankful for and searching for the splendid focuses in your day. Shift thinking, and you'll begin the day empowered.

7. Overscheduling and Over-Engagement.

People tend to underestimate how long things take with so many things to do. This habit of overscheduling and over-engagement can quickly lead to burn out. Always ensure that you permit extra time and energy for the unforeseen. Take regular breaks and don't overcommit to other people. This gives you more freedom for yourself and you won't be running the risk of letting others down by not turning up. Try not to overestimate what you can complete, so you won't feel like a disappointment. Be sensible and practical with your scheduling. Unexpectedly and eventually, you'll complete more.

8. Postponing or Discarding the Tough Tasks.

We have a restricted measure of mental energy, and as we exhaust this energy, our dynamic and efficiency decrease quickly. This is called decision exhaustion. Running the bad habit of postponing and disregarding the tough tasks will trigger this reaction in us. At the point when you put off extreme assignments till late in the day because they're scary, you deplete more and more of your mental resources. To beat choice weariness, you should handle complex assignments toward the beginning of the day when your brain is new.

9. Failure To Prioritize Your Self-Care.

Work, family commitments, and generally talking of the general obligations give almost everyone an awesome excuse to let your self-care rehearses pass by the wayside. Achievement-oriented minds of individuals see how basic self-care is to their expert achievement. Invest energy doing things that bring you delight and backing your psychological and actual wellbeing. "Success" doesn't exclusively apply to your finances or expert accomplishments.

10. Waiting for the Easier Way Out / Waiting for the Perfect Hack of Your Life.

The most noticeably awful everyday habit is trusting that things will occur and for a chance to thump at your entryway. As such, you become an inactive onlooker, not a proactive part of your own life. Once in a while, it shows itself as the quest for simple little-known techniques. Rather than getting down to work, ineffective individuals search how to take care of job quicker for quite a long time. Try not to begin with a #lifehack search on the internet unless it really does improve your productivity without sacrificing the necessary steps you need to take each day to achieve holistic success.

✓ Merging It All Together

A portion of these habits may appear to be minor, yet they add up. Most amount to an individual decision between immediate pleasures and enduring ones. The most exceedingly awful propensity is forgetting about what matters to you. Always remember that you are just one habit away from changing you life forever.

Chapter 7:

8 Ways To Adopt New Thoughts That Will Be Beneficial To Your Life

"Each morning we are born again. What we do today is what matters most." - Buddha

Is your glass half-empty or half-full? Answering this age-old question may reflect your outlook on life, your attitude toward yourself, whether you're optimistic or pessimistic, or it may even affect your health. Studies show that personality traits such as optimism and pessimism play a considerable role in determining your health and well-being. The positive thinking that comes with optimism is a practical part of stress management. Positive thinking in no way means that we keep our heads in the sand and ignore life's less pleasant situations. Instead, you have to approach the unpleasantness more positively and productively. Always think that something best is going to happen, and ignore the worst-case scenarios.

Here are some ways for you to adopt new thoughts that will benefit your outlook on life.

1. Breaking Out Old Thinking Patterns

We all can get stuck in a loop of specific thoughts. Sure, they may look comfortable on the outside, but we don't realize that these thoughts are what's holding us back most of the time. It's crucial to let fresh ideas and thoughts into your life and break away from the negative ones to see new paths ahead. We could start by challenging our assumptions in every situation. We may already assume what's about to happen if we fall into some condition, but trying new preconceptions can open up some exciting possibilities for us.

2. Rephrase The Problem

Your creativity can get limited by how you define or frame your problems. If you keep on looking at the problem from one side only, chances are you won't get much exposure to the solution. Whereas, if you look at it in different ways and different angles, new solutions can emerge. For example, the founder of Uber, Garret Camp, could have focused on buying and managing enough vehicles for him to make a profit. Instead, he looked more into how he could best entertain the passengers and thus, made a powerful app for their comfort.

3. Think In Reverse

Try turning the problem upside-down if you're having difficulties finding a new approach. Flip the situation and explore the opposite of what you want to achieve. This can help you present innovative ways to tackle the real issue. If you're going to take a good picture, try all of its angles first so you can understand which grade will be more suitable and which angles you should avoid. If you want to develop a new design for your website, try its worst look first and then make it the exact opposite. Apply different types of creativity to tackle your problems.

4. Make New Connections

Another way to generate new ideas and beneficial thoughts is by making unique and unexpected connections. Some of the best ideas click to you by chance, you hear or see something utterly unconnected to the situation you're trying to solve, and an idea has occurred to you almost instantly. For instance, architect Mick Pearce developed a groundbreaking climate-control system by taking the concept from the self-cooling mounds built by termites. You can pick on any set of random words, picture prompts, and objects of interest and then look for the novel association between them and your problem.

5. Finding Fresh Perspectives

Adding extra dynamism to your thinking by taking a step back from your usual standpoint and viewing a problem through "fresh eyes" might be beneficial for you to tackle an issue and give new thoughts. You could also talk to someone with a different perspective, life experience, or cultural background and would be surprised to see their approach. Consider yourself being the other person and see life from their eyes, their point of view.

6. Focus On The Good Things

Challenges and struggles are a part of life. When you're faced with obstacles, try and focus on the good part, no matter how seemingly insignificant or small it seems. If you keep looking for it, you will definitely find the proverbial silver lining in every cloud if it's not evident in the beginning.

7. Practice Gratitude

Practicing gratitude is said to reduce stress, foster resilience, and improve self-esteem. If you're going through a bad time, think of people, moments, or things that bring you some kind of comfort and happiness and express your gratitude once in a while. This could be anything, from thanking your loved one to lending a helping hand to anyone.

8. Practice Positive Self-Talk

We sometimes are our own worst critics and tend to be the hardest on ourselves. This can cause you to form a negative opinion of yourself. This could be prevented by practicing positive self-talk. As a result, this could influence your ability to regulate your feelings, thoughts, and behaviors under stress.

Conclusion

Developing a positive attitude can help you in many ways than you might realize. When you practice positive thinking, you consciously or subconsciously don't allow your mind to entertain any negative thoughts. You will start noticing remarkable changes all around you. By reducing your self-limiting beliefs, you will effectively grow as you have never imagined before. You can change your entire outlook on life by harnessing the power of positive thinking. You will also notice a significant boost in your confidence.

Chapter 8:

How To Stop Procrastinating

Procrastination; perhaps the most used word of our generation. Procrastination can range from a minor issue that hurts your productivity or a significant issue that's preventing you from achieving your goals. You feel powerless, and you feel hopeless; you feel de-motivated, De-strategized, even guilty and ashamed, but all in vain.

Let me in all of you on a secret of life, the need to avoid pain and the desire to gain pleasure. That is what we consider the two driving forces of life. Repeat this mantra till it gets in the back of your head. And if you don't take control over these two forces, they'll take control over you and your entire life. The need to avoid pain is what gets us into procrastinating. We aren't willing to step out of our comfort zone, be uncomfortable, fear the pain of spending our energies, fear failure, embarrassment, and rejection. We don't simply procrastinate because there's no other choice; we procrastinate because whatever it is, we don't consider it essential to us. It's not that something meaningful for us or urgent to us, and when something doesn't feel binding to us, we tend to put it off. We link to link a lot of pain to not taking action. But what if we reversed the roles? What if we start to connect not taking action to be more painful than taking action. We have to change our perspective.

See that the long-term losses of not taking action are 1000x more painful than the short-term losses of taking those actions.

Stop focusing on the short-term pain of spending your time, energy, and emotions on the tasks at hand. START focusing on the long-term pain that comes when you'll realize you're not even close to the goals you were meant to achieve.

Stop your desire to gain pleasure from the unnecessary and unimportant stuff. You would rather skip your workout to watch a movie instead. You're focusing on the pleasure, the meaningless short-term craving that'll do you no good. Imagine the pleasure we'd gain if we actually did that workout. Stop making excuses for procrastinating. Start owning up to yourself, your tasks, your goals. Set a purpose in your life and start working tirelessly towards it. Take breaks but don't lose your focus!

If you're in school and you're not getting the grades that you want, and still you're not doing anything about it, then maybe it's not a priority for you. But how do we make it meaningful? How do we make it purposeful? You need to find that motivation to get yourself going. And I promise you once you find that purpose, you'll get up early in the morning, and you'll start working to make your dreams come true.

Don't just talk about it, be about it! You were willing to graduate this year, you were willing to go to the gym and change your physique, you were willing to write that book, but what happened? You didn't make them a priority, and you eventually got tired of talking. Take a deep breath and allow yourself to make the last excuse there is that's stopping you from whatever it is that you're supposed to do. I don't have enough money; I don't write well, I don't sing well, I don't have enough knowledge, that's it. That's the last excuse you're going to make and get it over with. Aren't you tired of feeling defeated? Aren't you tired of getting beat? Aren't you tired of saying "I'll get it done soon" over and over again? To all the procrastinators, YOU. STILL. HAVE. PLENTY. OF. TIME. Don't quit, don't give up, don't just lay there doing nothing; you can make it happen. But not with that procrastinating. Set up a goal, tear it into manageable pieces, stop talking about the things you were going to do, and start doing them for real!

It's not too late for anything. There might be some signs that'll show you that you need to rest. Take them. Take the time you need to get back on track. But don't give up on the immediate gratification. Don't listen to that little voice in your head. Get out of bed, lift those weights, start working on that project, climb that mountain. You're the only person that's stopping you from achieving your goals, your dreams. With long-term success, either you're going to kick the hell out of life, or life's going to kick the hell out of you; whichever of that happens the most will become your reality. We're the master of our fates, the ambassador of our ambitions; why waste our time and lives away into doing something that won't even matter to us in a few years? Why not work towards something that will touch people, inspire them, give them hope.

I'll do it in the next hour, I'll do it the next day, I'll do it the next week, and before you know, you're dragging it to the next month or even next year. And that's the pain of life punching you in the face. The regrets of missing opportunities will eventually catch up to you. Every day you get a chance to either make the most out of life or sit on the sidelines taking the crumbles which people are leaving behind. Take what you want or settle for what's left! That's your choice.

You have to push yourself long past the point of boredom. Boredom is your worst enemy. It kills more people in the pursuit of success than anything or anyone will ever destroy. Your life just doesn't stop accidentally. It's a series of actions that you either initiate or don't initiate. Some people have already made their big decisions today, after waking up. While some, they're still dwelling on the things that don't matter. They're afraid of self-evaluation, thus wasting their time. So focus on yourself, focus on what you're doing with your time, have clarity on what you're trying to achieve. Build into what you're trying to accomplish. Between where you are and where you want to go, there's a skill set that you have to master. There's a gap that's asking for your hard work. So pay the price for what you want to become.

Chapter 9:

<u>10 Habits of Millionaires</u>

Millionaires are people who own quite a substantial amount of wealth. They have passed both the hundreds and thousands threshold and are moving towards the billion mark. They have common habits that a majority of them subscribe to.

Here are ten habits of millionaires:

1. <u>They Are Ever Busy</u>

Millionaires have upgraded from the thousands category over quite some time during which they worked day and night to increase their wealth portfolio. This has made them learn to be busy for a better part of their life.

They are busy strategizing on how they can make it to the next level and they do not have the luxury to relax. They are in a constant race against time and how they can make their businesses do better.

2. <u>They Prioritize the Management of Their Property</u>

Millionaires have vast wealth ranging from commercial and residential houses, vehicles, and land among other properties. They need to be extra vigilant on how they manage all their assets lest they lose them.

Sometimes they need to hire professionals to help them in management. Millionaires prioritize this because their property is their fortress and source of financial muscle. Moreover, they have a legal counsel to guide them not to transgress the law.

3. They Have A Diversified Investment Portfolio

Millionaires have invested heavily in every sector of the economy. They diversify their investment to cushion them from economic shocks like the one that gripped global economies during the coronavirus pandemic.

This habit has made millionaires stay afloat despite economic depressions. It is a survival mechanism that you need to adapt if you also want to be a millionaire. Regardless of how better one economic sector performs, do not over-invest in it.

4. They Are Risk-Takers

Like gamblers, millionaires are risk-takers. Their risk appetite is insatiable. It is very difficult to talk them out of it. They can stake a portion of their investment and be ready to win it all or lose it all. Sometimes this habit pays off and that is what distinguishes them from common people.

However, millionaires curb their risk appetite by seeking the advice of risk managers. They are advised whether or not an investment is viable before they commit to it. You should make calculated risk moves if you want a financial breakthrough. This is the lifestyle of millionaires.

5. They Are Hardworking

How do you think millionaires got there in the first place? It is through hard work and a lot of sacrifices. They have had to endure early mornings and late nights for them to achieve their current successes. It is not an easy journey to embark on.

Hard work sets them apart from those who want to reap in fields they have not planted. It is only fair for millionaires to harvest the fruits of their hard work. Begin working hard tirelessly until your efforts bear fruits.

6. They Are Disciplined

Hard work propels you to the top but discipline will maintain you there. Millionaires are disciplined in the use of their resources. They can account for every coin they spend. Such a level of financial discipline is rare and difficult to come by. This is what makes them stand out. When you lead a disciplined life, you do not engage in activities that endanger your growth. The reason why millionaires grow while common people maintain the status quo is because the former are disciplined, unlike the latter who are easily tossed to and fro. Discipline is the key to seal your success.

7. They Verify Facts

Quite a few people would go a step further to verify what they are told. Millionaires do not take information at face value. They take the trouble to check the authenticity of their sources of information. It can be very disastrous if they act on heresy.

The businesses of millionaires could collapse if the public see its directors as untrustworthy. Gossip, rumors, and heresy do not build empires. Maintain an unassailable reputation like millionaires if you want to grow like them.

8. They Have Thick Skin

Millionaires have risen to who they are because they did not listen to every voice that talked to them. They were sometimes talked out of decisions they made but they did not give in. At other times they were insulted by people they least expected but they remained steadfast.

You need to develop a thick skin like millionaires if you want to progress. Critics should not have the power to shout you to silence. Be like millionaires who will overlook the negativity of their critics and rise above their resistance.

9. They Are United

Millionaires are very united in their circles. They maintain close fellowship with fellow millionaires and never hesitate to come through for one another during hard times. This type of unity is rare in common people.

The unity of millionaires is to be emulated. This habit makes them stand out in society. United we stand, divided we fall. In their unity, millionaires protect their interests. In the absence of unity, they would all wither away like petals of a flower.

10. They Practice Corporate Social Responsibility

In the spirit of giving back to society, millionaires do corporate social responsibility in many ways. Through their companies and foundations, they build schools and hospitals for the community. It is how they express their gratitude to society.

There are tens, even hundreds of beneficiaries of acts of charity from millionaires. This has made it difficult for society to turn against millionaires because they also benefit from their businesses.

In conclusion, millionaires have these ten habits that distinguish them from others. Develop them slowly and watch yourself fit in their shoes.

Chapter 10:

Stop Lying To Yourself

What do you think you are doing with your life? What do you keep on telling everyone you are up to? What ambitions do you make for yourself? What ideas do you follow? What goals do you want to follow and do you really have no choice in any of these?

These are not some random rude questions one might ask you. Because you deserve all of them if you still don't have anything meaningful in your life to stand behind.

You need to find a real achievement in your life that can make you feel accomplished.

Life is always a hard race to finish line with all of us running for the same goal of glory and success. But not all of us have the thing that will get us to that line first. SO when we fail to get there, we make reasons for our failure.

The reality is that it is never OK to make excuses for your failure when you weren't even eligible to join others to start with.

You have been lying to yourself this whole time, telling yourself that you have everything that takes to beat everyone to that finish line!

You have been lying to yourself saying that you are better than anyone there who came well prepared!

You keep telling yourself that you have a better understanding of things that you have just seen in your life for the first time! That you have a better approach towards life. That you know the best way to solve any problem.

Well, guess what my friend, You are wrong!

You don't have it all in you, you never did and you would probably never will. Because no man can master even one craft, let alone every. You need to do your homework for everything in your life, you try to master everything you come across but you can never really do so because you are a human. It is humanly impossible to be perfect at everything.

So stop calling yourself a saint or a self-taught genius because you are not.

You have this habit of lying to yourself because you find an escape from your faults. You find a way to cope with your inabilities. You find a way to soothe yourself that you are not wrong, just because everyone else says so.

You have to understand the fact that life has a way to be lived, and it is never the way of denial. It is rather the hopeful and quiet way of living your life with hard work and freedom.

You have to make your life worth living for. Because you know it in the back of your head that you have done the necessary hard work before to be able to compete among the best of the best out there.

You must have a strong feeling of justice towards yourself and towards others that makes you feel deserving of the highest honors and the biggest riches. Because you worked your whole life to be able to stand here and be a nominee for what life has to offer the best

Chapter 11:

<u>10 Habits of Kobe Bryant</u>

Throughout 20 seasons, the late Kobe Bryant earned a reputation as the greatest basketball player of all time with the Los Angeles Lakers. The six-foot-six shooting guard dominated the court in NBA history, winning five NBA titles, a record of 18 consecutive All-Star Game selections, four All-Star Game MVP Awards, and the Academy Award for Best Animated Short Film, "Dear Basketball."

Bryant's off-court legacy was similarly outstanding, with record earnings for an NBA player, winning investments, and a lucrative shoe deal that increased his net worth to more than $600 million. He was also renowned for his strong work ethic. Highly applauded, you'll find endless stories on his 20-year career work ethics from his teammates, competitors, coaches, and other acquaintances.

Here are 10 Kobe Bryant's habits.

1. His Work Ethics

Kobe Bryant was well-known for having a solid work ethic. If he ever lost a game, he could figure out why and spend extra time improving. Losing a shot for Kobe meant training for hours and days until he couldn't miss it anymore. He was going to train so hard that you wouldn't beat him.

2. Become Obsessive

Kobe not only obsessed on basketball, but also dedicated his energy on becoming the best in every manner. "If you want to be exceptional at something, you have to obsess over it," he once said. That's precisely the mind set you need if you want to be the best in your field. Embrace your obsession, fall in love with the process, and use it to reach heights that others cannot.

3. Mamba Attitude

Kobe was determined to be one of the greatest basketballers at only 13 years of age. He said in an interview that he was inspired by great players like Michael Jordan and Magic Jordan. He would watch them play and wonder, "Can I get to that level?" "i don't know," he could say, "but let's find out." Whether you're starting a business, becoming a great athlete, learning a new skill, or forming a new habit, modelling your habits after someone who has already succeeded will save you the most time and money in the long run.

4. Compete Against Yourself

When you compete with yourself, you put others in the position to keep up with you. Kobe never had this problem because he fought within him to be the type of athlete who could win more after winning his first championship. Throughout his career, he progressed from being the No. 8 Kobe who wanted to win to the No. 24 Kobe who needed to be a leader and a better teammate.

5. Embracing New Abilities

After Kobe retired from sports in 2016, his next focus was on finding ways to inspire the world through diverse stories, characters, and leadership. He pushed and founded multimedia production company Granity Studios, which is 2018, lead to his Academy Award- a Sports Emmy and an Annie Award for his short animated film Dear Basketball. Embracing new skills will keep your legacy going and diversify your abilities in different walks of life.

6. Leaders develop leaders

"I enjoyed testing people and making them uncomfortable," Kobe once said. "That is what leads to introspection, which leads to improvement. I guess you could say I challenged them to be their best selves." On the court, Kobe was a strong, albeit contentious, leader for his team.

7. Handling the Pressure is Everything

When you're under pressure, you're forced to make critical choices and decisions. Sometimes, you'll make the wrong decisions, but that what keeps you going strong. When Kobe was playing against the Utah Jazz at 18 years, he missed a shot which led to his team losing the game. This had him working on the shot during the entire off-season.

8. Perseverance

Kobe's success was as a result of sticking to his process through perseverance. He was determined not to give in to anyone or anything that pushed him backwards. Your strength to keep moving will eventually payoff.

9. Failure Begets Growth

Failure is only ideal when you keep learning. In an interview, Kobe mentioned being an 11-year-old basketball player who played in a summer league for an entire season without scoring a single point! Really?! So he had to work extra for the following ten months to become a better shot and learn how to score.

10. Passion Is Everything

It's undeniable that Kobe had a strong love and enthusiasm for basketball. His passion for basketball, his work ethic, and competitiveness helped him become a five-time champion. When you sincerely love your craft, and put more into it, you will always rise against the odds to achieve success.

Conclusion

Although Bryant was an exceptional talent, his success was a product of an intense, obsessive work ethic. Bryant's desire to be the best was evident in almost every aspect of his life.

Chapter 12:

<u>10 Habits That Will Ruin Your Life</u>

A habit is an automated response or reaction to issues. Habits do not just develop overnight, they grow roots over time and it becomes difficult to get rid of them. Some habits are very good since they help us become better versions of ourselves, but some are toxic and you need to get rid of them as soon as possible. We simply cannot ignore the power of habits in our lives, good or bad. Habits have the ability to shape our futures, either in a positive way or a negative way.

Here are 10 habits that will ruin your life if you're not careful:

1.   Procrastination.

The simple small things in our routine are the building blocks of chronic addictive habits in our lives. They may seem negligible but if left unattended, can turn out to be major nuisances.

Would you even imagine, for example, how a simple act like procrastination could lock you out of a once-in-a-lifetime opportunity? Why should you do something later when you can do it now? With a little bit of introspection, find out what puts you off from acting later instead of now. Procrastination could potentially breed laziness which in turn shuts every door of success in our lives. Aim to resolve your habit of procrastination by implementing incentives to act now.

2. Bad attitude.

A bad attitude is like a flat tire; if you do not change it, you will not go anywhere. This gives us the insight of how powerful bad attitude can slow our momentum in life. Having a positive attitude in everything goes a long way to help us interact better with potential clients and employers. It pays to see things from a better perspective. Yes, there is a problem at work, but instead of focusing on the problem, focus on the solution to it. After all, who will want to be around a pessimist always? A bad attitude will attract friends of the same character. With such company, our vision of the future is limited. We will definitely not be making any progress.

3. Impulse decision making.

In his book *Economic warfare: Secrets of wealth creation in the Age of Welfare politics,* Ziad K. Abdelnour says "Do not promise when you are happy, do not reply when you are angry, and do not decide when you are sad." This is because most decisions made in the heat of the moment are superficial. Continuously making impulse decisions will land you in less than ideal situations and the damage caused could be irreparable. Carefully consider every possible scenario at play before arriving at decisions. Make that routine your shield against poor decision-making.

4. Underestimating issues.

As a rule of the thumb, never under estimate your enemy. Treating every opponent as worthy of a challenge will remove pitfalls in your battlefield. The moment you choose to live in a bubble, you lose contact with reality. It is one thing to underestimate something only once, and it is another thing to constantly underestimate them. This disadvantages you from rationally analyzing matters that come your way. Not only will you attract ridicule, but also the consequences that come with it. Professionally, you may cost your organization or client a fortune. That is the last thing you want to be doing right now.

5. Oversleeping

The importance of sleep in our lifestyle is incomparable. This is not the same with oversleeping. It denies you the time to be productive, either at work or at home. Again, sleeping unnecessarily encourages reluctance (a polite name for laziness). It is a liability for everyone in the end. It is preferable to have a routine sleeping schedule that you adhere to religiously. An alarm when it is bedtime and when it is time to wake up. It will help you manage your time and discourage oversleeping.

6. Failure To Plan

It sounds cliché but it is true that failure to plan is planning to fail. The failure to plan is not ignorable. Even without people knowing, it is a common problem to many. They classify it as a managerial routine task but it is not entirely true. Planning is for everybody who wants to use the resources available to them optimally. You will notice a change in your lifestyle, however minimal, when you start planning for everything (at least what is humanly possible).

7. Poor Eating Habits

We are what we eat. We do not eat solely because we are hungry, but also because we need to be healthy. The food we eat plays a major role on our health status. Our routine activities are also dependent on our health status. We cannot work effectively when we are hungry, can we? It is not uncommon for people to find quick solutions to satisfy their hunger. They go for fast foods and drinks that will satiate their hunger for the moment until sometime later when they can have a proper meal. Are you one of them? Kindly desist. Eating healthy foods will also keep lifestyle diseases away. It is a win-win for everyone.

8. Being Too Lazy For Anything

Whether it is the act of getting work done or going to the gym, laziness is whole other ballgame that could potentially ruin our lives if we're careful. It may be worse than procrastination because at least in that regard you are still doing the thing you set out to do eventually. Being too lazy and completely forgoing work and exercise for days could lead to a downward spiral. The more we succumb to laziness the stronger it becomes and the harder it becomes to get back on track towards our health and work goals. Nip laziness in the bud by resisting the urge to think, just do. Doing is the first step to the path you always wanted to be on.

9. Not Being Organised

It is easy for us to fall into the bad habit of not organizing our things, cleaning our dishes, and misplacing our items. When we invite clutter into our living space it is most likely that it will spread to other areas of our lives as well. A cluttered mind, cluttered relationship, cluttered sense of self are potential ways to confuse the road ahead for you. You may start making poor decisions that could affect all aspects of your well-being.

10. Getting Addicted On Substances

This one most likely speaks for itself. The more we fall into the habit of turning to substances such as alcohol, cigarettes, hard or soft drugs, is the time we are going on a downward spiral. Nothing good can come from taking these substances instead of dealing with the problems we have head on. Drowning our sorrows using these methods can definitely become a life-long addiction. If we're not careful we may never be able to claw out of it alive. As much as possible seek resolutions to the problems in your lives with friends, family, or even therapy if needed. It can definitely save you from a lot of pain and suffering.

Be careful not to let these 10 habits get in the way of a happy and healthy life. As much as possible rid these habits and adopt positive ones that can move your life in the direction that you've always wanted.

Chapter 13:

Doing The Thing You Love Most

Today we are going to talk about following your heart and just going for your passion, even if it ends up being a hobby project.

Many of us have passions that we want to pursue. Whether it be a sport, a fitness goal, a career goal, or simply just doing something we know we are good at. Something that electrifies our soul. Something that really doesn't require much persuasion for us to just go do it on a whim.

Many of us dare not pursue this passion because people have told us time and time again that it will not lead to anywhere. Or maybe it is that voice inside your head that is telling you you should just stick to the practical things in life. Whatever the reasons may be, that itch always seem to pester us, calling out to us, even though we have tried our best to put it aside.

We know what our talents are, and the longer we don't put it out there in the world, the longer we keep it bottled up inside of us, the longer the we will regret it. Personally, Music has always been something that has been calling out to me since i was 15. I've always dabbled in and out of it, but never took it seriously. I found myself 14 years later, wondering how much i could've achieved in the music space if i had just leaned in to it just a little.

I decided that I had just about put it off for long enough and decided to pursue music part time. I just knew deep down inside me that if i did not at least try, that i was going to regret it at some point again in the future. It is true that passions come and go. We may jump from passion to passion over the course of our lives, and that is okay. But if that thing has been there calling out to you for years or even decades, maybe you should pay closer attention to it just a little more.

Make your passion a project. Make it a hobby. Pursue it in one form or another. We may never be able to make full careers out of our passions, but we can at least incorporate it into our daily lives like a habit. You may find ourselves happier and more fulfilled should you tap that creative space in you that has always been there.

Sure life still takes precedence. Feeding the family, earning that income, taking care of that child. But never for one second think that you should sacrifice doing what truly makes you happy for all of that other stuff, no matter how important. Even as a hobby, pursuing it maybe 30mins a day, or even just an hour a week. It is a start and it is definitely better than nothing.

At the end of the day passions are there to feed our soul. To provide it will some zest and life to our otherwise mundane lives. The next time you hear that voice again, lean in to it. Don't put it off any longer.

Chapter 14:

<u>The Power of Developing Eye Contact with Your Client</u>

We've all heard the age-old saying the "eyes are the window to the soul," and in many ways, it holds. Everybody knows looking others in the eyes is beneficial in communication, but how important is eye contact, and how is it defined?

Eye contact can be subtle or even obvious. It can be a glaring scowl when a person is upset or a long glance when we see something off about someone else's appearance. It can even be a direct look when we are trying to express a crucial idea.

1) Respect

In Western countries like the United States, eye contact is critical to show and earn respect. From talking to your boss on the job or thanking your mom for dinner, eye contact shows the other person that you feel equal in importance.

There are other ways to show respect, but our eyes reflect our sincerity, warmth, and honesty.

This is why giving and receiving eye contact while talking is a surefire sign of a good conversation. Nowadays, it's common for people to glance at their phones no matter if they're in the middle of a conversation or not. That's why eye contact will set you apart and truly show that you give them your full and undivided attention.

2) Understanding

Sometimes locking glances is the only sign you need to show someone that you understand what they are talking about. More specifically, if you need to get a vital point across, eye contact is the best way to communicate that importance. Eye contact is also a form of background acknowledgment like saying "yeah" and "mhmm."

That means it shows the speaker that you are tuned in to and understand what they are saying.

3) Bonding

When someone is feeling an emotion or just performing a task, the same neurons that shine in their brain light up in someone else's brain who is watching them. This is because we have "mirror neurons" in our brains that are very sensitive to facial expressions and, most importantly, eye contact.

Direct eye contact is so powerful that it increases empathy and links together emotional states. Never underestimate the power of eye contact in creating long-lasting bonds.

4) Reveal Thoughts and Feelings

We have countless ways of describing eyes, including "shifty-eyed," "kind-eyed," "bright-eyed," "glazed over," and more. It's no wonder just about every classic love story starts with "two pairs of eyes meeting across the room." Eye contact is also a powerful form of simultaneous communication, meaning you don't have to take turns doing the communicating.

Ever wonder why poker players often wear sunglasses inside? It's because "the eyes don't lie." We instinctually look into people's eyes from birth to try and understand what they are thinking, and we continue to do it for life.

Chapter 15:

Stop Ignoring Your Health

Do you have a busy life? Do you follow a hard and continuous regime of tasks every day for a significant amount of time? Have you ever felt that you cannot enjoy even the happiest moments of your life even if you want to? Let me highlight one reason you might recognize it straight away. You are not enjoying your days while still being in all your senses because you don't have your mind and body in the right place.

All these years you have lived your life as a race. You have taken part in every event in and around your life just because you never wanted to miss anything. But in this process, you never lived your life to its full potential. You never lived a single moment with just the emotional intention of being then and there and not trying to live it like just another day or event.

People often get so busy with making their careers that they don't realize what is more important in life? It is their mental and physical health!

You will not get anywhere far in your life if you keep ignoring the signs of sickness your body keeps giving you. Your body is a machine with a conditional warranty. The day you violate the conditions of this warranty, life will become challenging and you won't even be interested in the basic tasks at hand.

You might have heard the famous saying that "Health is Wealth". Let it sink in for a while and analyze your own life. You don't need to be a top-tier athlete to have a good body. You need a good body for your organs to work properly. You need an active lifestyle to be more productive and be more present and engaged in the things that are going around you.

The dilemma of our lives is that we don't care about what we have right now, but we care a lot about what we want. Not realizing that what we want might be cursed but what we have is the soul of good living. And that my friends are the blessing of health that most of us take for granted.

Most people have a tendency and devotion to work specifically on their health and fitness on a priority basis. They have a better standard of life. These people have a clearer mind to feel and capture the best moments in life with what their senses can offer best to them.

If you don't stop ignoring your health, you won't ever get out of this constant struggle. The struggle to find the reasons for you being detached from everything despite being involved every time.

Being careful and observant of your health doesn't make you selfish. This makes you a much more caring person because not only your life but the life of others around you is also affected by your sickness. Not only your resources are used for your treatments but the attention and emotions of your loved ones are also being spent, just in hope of your wellness.

Chapter 16:

How Ditching Your Phone Can Make You Happier

Where is your smartphone at present? Odds are it is close to you, and on the off chance that it vibrates or dings, you will quit perusing this article and verify who messaged you or what occurred on Twitter. Perhaps you remember you're dependent on your smartphone and all that accompanies it, or possibly you don't believe it's something awful to be continually associated with. Regardless, if your smartphone is always with you and always looking at it, you could utilize a break. Unplugging from social media and innovation is frightening for many individuals; however, it doesn't need to be. It could be a truly extraordinary encounter.

Here's why.

Technology has made it simple for individuals to reach others every minute of every day, for better or worse. Your friend can call at 2 a.m. at the point when she needs a ride home, yet your supervisor can likewise call at 10 p.m. at the point when he needs you to assemble into a conference — presently. You can reconnect with old friends from secondary school, yet your greatest enemy is continually posting her most recent achievements, causing you to feel less and inadequate.

The surge of texts, notifications, emails, and calls implies your mind is consistently on high alarm, sitting tight for the next ding. You can never genuinely unwind, except if your telephone is off. Believe it or not. Not on vibrate, off. By turning your phone off for even 20 minutes, you can give your cerebrum, body, and feelings a break from the consistent commitment. You can zero in on the book you're perusing, give your cherished ones your full focus, completely appreciate the film you're watching and shut your brain off when you're attempting to rest.

Numerous individuals have had a go at unplugging, regardless of whether it be for five minutes or a whole year. While a few groups say from the outset, they felt restless and disrupted, they, at last, started to see the value in the time to themselves. There's no commitment to answer your cell phone when you don't hear it ring, no strain to "like" your dearest companion's latest status when you didn't see it. Moving back from these "responsibilities" allows you an opportunity to truly be with yourself or with your loved ones. With your cellphone on, a piece of you is consistent with individuals posting on Snapchat and messaging you. With no time really for yourself, you can begin to feel excessively pushed or discouraged.

Chapter 17:

Never Give Up – 3 Reasons to Carry on Believing in Yourself During Dark Times

We all have black moments. Sometimes these stretch into days, weeks and even months. Both small and huge problems can quickly overwhelm us. There are many reasons.

When we are really down, it may begin to feel like we are living a lifetime of hell. We get caught up in a swirling torrent of negativity. Light and hope fade. Emotionally and psychologically, we become spent. At the extreme, we might even begin to tell ourselves that we will never achieve success, happiness and joy ever again.

Avoiding sinking deeper and deeper into an unpleasant pit of despair can be avoided!

You need to recognize tipping points quickly. It is our cue to stop! Before you go down this rabbit hole, get proper perspective. The sooner the better. Think about it:

11. 1. Stop Focusing Predominantly on Others

Do you still primarily look for external validation? Constantly worrying. For example, what your father wanted you to become? What he thinks of you because you flunked out of university? What he is going to say now when he hears your boss said you are the worst sales performer this month! His views on you facing the horrible prospect of unemployment?

Everyone sees things differently. Actually, accepting we have very little control of what others think, feel and do is helpful. Making paramount what we think, feel and do about our life's direction and quality makes all the different. By doing this we no longer need anyone else's stamp of approval.

When we stop seeking others validation, we start seeking an authentic life. It suddenly becomes uniquely ours. Self-endorsement also feels good. Giving ourselves permission to take charge and chart our own course offers a sense of freedom. We begin to see clearly that at the end of the day, we are the best judges of our lives. It can become well lived on our terms. Let go of the rest.

12. 2.   Stop Believing Things Will Not Change

Past regrets aside, recognize you are in the here and now. Without that university degree you are never going to be that doctor your father wanted! However, you do have new options every moment. Seeing new and even creative opportunities during difficulties is the ultimate determinant of your ability to bounce back, turn things around and pursue a brighter future. Short of being fired or dying, there is still time to become the top sales person. It depends if you want it enough.

Think about the different periods, people and situations in your life. Each of us is living proof of constant change. We certainly can't stop the cycle of change. Our only option is really how we respond to the constant flow. Growth and progress are about making the most of change including obstacles and challenges. Often, we will deny the inevitability of change in an attempt to try avoid confronting our worst fears. We may fail. Again, and yet again. We need to find the courage to go for it irrespective.

Committing to the idea that embracing change gives us another opportunity to get better and learn. Current results are temporary and stepping stones.

1. 3. Stop Not Seeing Your Worth

When important people in our lives tell us that we are not good enough, it can be earth shattering. When we tell ourselves, we are not good enough, this is outright dangerous. Especially so if we are astute enough to know that the most significant opinion in our life is our own. Any lack of self-worth limits potential to come out undamaged from dark periods. We can get over the bosses' views that we will never cut it as a high-flying sales guru. But it becomes impossible to lift ourselves up and see the light when we forget our own brilliance and essence. We must self-affirm to create self-love. We need to know our worth even when others miss it.

It is a crucial part of life's journey to find one's true self. This can mean deciding to change a sales career at any point, including to that of a life as a nomad. We need to make choices that maximize our sense of self-worth, not erode it. There is no prescribe perfect life trajectory. Once we can measure ourselves as much for our internal achievements, as by our external achievements in the world, we would have found hidden treasure. Self-worth is the cornerstone of mental health and stability. Block by block we can build this foundation as a fortress against any and all negative onslaughts that come our way.

So, if we remain focused on these 3 important thoughts, we will strengthen our innate ability to survive whatever life throws our way. Resilience becomes our armor as we conquer our demons. Whatever shape or size they may appear in. We are ready.

Chapter 18:

Why You Need To Find Your Why

Your why is your reason for being.

Your reason for living.

Your reason for acting.

Without a why life begins to feel demoralising.

Without a purpose, what is the purpose?

What chance do you think you have of achieving anything, without a reason?

Go out and ask 20 people why they are working, apart from the pay.

Roughly 16 will not be able to give you a clear answer, and 4 will.

The 4 that will have a plan and a goal to achieve more.

They probably already are more successful than the 16 with no answer.

The 4 know their current work is just a step to a bigger goal.

They know their what and their why behind everything they are doing.

The 16 just landed in that job by chance and will probably never leave it.

They may progress up the company ladder slowly,

But with no clear reason to achieve anything greater they will stay where they are, in perceived security.

Do you know why you are doing what you are doing?

If not, it's about time you discover your why.

It may be to providing a better life for your family and friends.

Your motives may be financial, they may not.

Maybe your why is to lead a less stressful life.

Maybe that means your require less money to be happy.

Your reason is individual and personal.

No one else should influence that.

Seek to heed advice from people who are where you want to be in life.

You wouldn't let a mechanic perform surgery on you,

so why would you accept advice on success from the unsuccessful.

They may be successful in their field.

But if their field is not your field, they have no business telling you how to play.

Their why is not your why, and their what is not your what.

If the goals and reasons are different, the advice is irrelevant.

Politely respect their advice.

Use their success to fuel your drive for success in your own field.

Help it guide you to a similar path that you are aiming towards.

Your why is so important.

It will be the reason you persist when things get tough.

If you have no clearly defined reason, it becomes easy for you to quit.

A clearly defined goal (your what),

and a clearly defined reason (your why),

are critical to any lasting happiness and success.

Without them you are just aimlessly drifting from nothing to nothing.

Without clearly defining the terms of your life , you forfeit the power of

your will and your life will be decided by someone else.

That is tragedy.

Your why truly is everything on the path to achieving your what.

Your end goal.

Your dream life.

Everything that you will sit down and clearly define.

The detail of everything and the people who will enjoy it - your ultimate

why.

What and why go together like salt and pepper or bread and butter.

You can't have one without the other.

Chapter 19:

Stop Setting The Wrong Goals

Setting the wrong goals will lead to disappointment in success.

Chances are you are aiming too low and

will not be satisfied with the outcome.

The outcome and the reason for

it must be clear before you begin.

Will the result make you satisfied?

Will you enjoy the journey to the result?

Your goal should encompass these questions

to make sure you are not setting the wrong goals.

You may be setting the wrong goals due to the expectations of others.

The goals you set should be personal to you -

something where you can enjoy the process and the result.

Is your goal likely to happen based on your current actions?

What could you do to make it more likely?

If you set the wrong goals you will end up doing a whole lot of work you

don't like doing for a result you don't want.

Start at the end in your mind.

What would the end result look, taste and feel like?

With that you can imagine the process.

Can you do that work?

Would you enjoy that work?

Or would the reality fall short of your current expectations.

Life is chess not checkers.

The grand masters of success play 10 years ahead.

Thinking about how their actions today will

influence their lives ten years from now .

What's your 10 year goal?

What are your first steps?

Start at the end and work it back to now in your mind.

If you can envision the goal and paths to it

the battle is half won and you will have clarity over your goals.

Setting the wrong goals decreases your motivation to attain them.

You can only attain your motivation if your why is strong enough.

What are you aiming for and why?

If your clarity is strong enough you will

feel the goal as if it is already real.

You can then confirm it is the right goal for you.

If you only feel half-hearted about something it is not for you

and it is probably a waste of your time.

It's better to go all out for something you really want

than to easily obtain something you don't.

The right goal for you will probably feel unrealistic at first.

People will probably tell you it is.

But you know that it really isn't.

If it's on your mind constantly then it

stands a good chance that it is the right goal for you.

You must think clearly about every aspect of your life

and the goal you wish to obtain.

Something that fits you and your true desires.

Your goal should be something that will make you happy as often as possible and give you the kind of financial life you want.

Never set goals because someone else thinks that is what you should be doing.

Only you know what you should be doing,

go after that and never accept anything less.

Gain clarity on your goals before you act.

Make sure it's something that will make you happy in the process and the results that come from it.

Chapter 20:
4 Ways to Deal with Feelings of Inferiority When Comparing to Others

When we're feeling inferior, it's usually a result of comparing ourselves to other people and feeling like we don't measure up. And let's be real, it happens all. The. Damn. Time. You could be scrolling through your Instagram feed, notice a new picture of someone you follow, and think: *Wow, how do they always look so perfect?! No amount of filters will make me look like that!* Or maybe you show up to a party, and you quickly realize you're in a room full of accomplished people with exciting lives, and the thought of introducing yourself sends you into a panic. Suddenly, you're glancing at the door and wondering what your best escape plan is. You could be meeting your partner's family for the first time, and you're worried that you won't fit in or that they'll think you're not good enough. You might feel easily intimidated by other people and constantly obsess over what they think of you, even though it's beyond your control.

Don't worry! We have some coping strategies for you that will help you work through your feelings. Try 'em out and see for yourself!

1. Engage in compassionate self-talk

When we feel inferior, we tend to pick ourselves apart and be hard on ourselves. Don't fall into the trap of being your own worst critic! Instead, build your <u>self-confidence</u> and self-esteem by saying positive things to yourself that resonate with you: *I'm feeling inferior right now, but I know my worth. I'm not defined by my credentials, my possessions, or my appearance. I am whole.*

2. Reach out for support or connect with a friend

Just like the Beatles song goes: *I get by with a little help from my friends!* Reach out to someone you can trust and who will be there for you. You might feel inferior now, but it doesn't mean you have to navigate it alone! Get all of those negative feelings off your chest. Having someone there to validate our feelings can be so helpful!

3. Give yourself a pep talk and utilize a helpful statement

Comparing ourselves to other people just brings down our mood and makes us feel like garbage. Sometimes, we gotta give ourselves a little pep talk to turn those negative thoughts around. *I feel inferior right now, but I can get through this! I'm not the only person who has felt this way, and I won't be the last. Everything is gonna be okay!*

4. Comfort yourself like a friend

If you don't have anyone who can be there for you at this moment, that's okay. You can be there for yourself! Think about how you would want a loved one to comfort you at this moment. Pat yourself on the back, treat yourself to some junk food, cuddle up on the couch with a warm, fuzzy blanket and binge your favorite show on Netflix. Be the friend you need right now!

Chapter 21:

Everything is A Marathon Not A Sprint

Ask your parents, what was it like to raise children till the time they were able to lift their weight and be self-sufficient. I am sure they will say, it was the most beautiful experience in their lives. But believe me, They are lying.

There is no doubt in it that what you are today is because of your parents, and your parents didn't rest on their backs while a nanny was taking care of you.

They spent countless nights of sleeplessness changing diapers and soothing you so that you can have a good night's sleep. They did that because they wanted to see a part of them grow one day and become what they couldn't be. What you are today is because of their continuous struggle over the years.

You didn't grow up overnight, and your parents didn't teach you everything overnight. It took years for them to teach you and it took even more time for you to learn.

This is life!

Life is an amalgamation of little moments and each moment is more important than the last one.

Start with a small change. Learn new skills. The world around you changes every day. Don't get stuck in your routine life. Expand your horizons. What's making you money today might not even exist tomorrow. So why stick to it for the rest of your life.

You are never too old to learn new things. The day you stop learning is the last day of your life. A human being is the most supreme being in this universe for a reason. That reason is the intellect and the ability to keep moving with their lives.

You can never be a millionaire in one night. It's a one-in-billion chance to win a lottery and do that overnight. Most people see the results of their efforts in their next generation, but the efforts do pay off.

If you want to have eternal success. It will take an eternity of effort and struggles to get there. Because life is a marathon and a marathon tests your last breaths. But when it pays off, it is the highest you can get.

Shaping up a rock doesn't take one single hit, but hundreds of precision cuts with keen observation and attention. Life is that same rock, only bigger and much more difficult.

Changing your life won't happen overnight. Changing the way you see things won't happen overnight. It will take time.

To know everything and to pretend to know everything is the wrong approach to life. It's about progress. It's about learning a little bit at each step along the way.

To evolve, to adapt, to figure out things as they come, is the process of life that every living being in this universe has gone through before and will continue to go through in the future. We are who we are because of the marathon of life.

Every one of us today has more powerful things in our possessions right now than our previous 4 generations combined. So we are lucky to be in this world, in this era.

We have unlimited resources at our disposal, but we still can't get things in the blink of an eye. Because no matter how evolved we are, we still are a slave to the reality of nature, and that reality is the time itself!

If you are taking each step to expect a treat at each stop, you might not get anything. But if you believe that each step that you take is a piece in a puzzle, a puzzle that becomes a picture that is far beautiful and meaningful, believe me, the sky is your limit.

Life is a set of goals. You push and grind to get these goals but when you get there you realize that there is so much more to go on and achieve.

Committing to a goal is difficult but watching your dreams come true is something worth fighting for.

You might not see it today, you might not see it 2 years from now, but the finish line is always one step closer. Life has always been and always will be a race to the top. But only the ones who make it to the top have gone through a series of marathons and felt the grind throughout everything.

Your best is yet to come but is on the other end of that finish line.

Chapter 22:

How to Hold Yourself Accountable For Everything That You Do

Staying on top of your work can be difficult without a manager over your shoulder. So how exactly do you manage yourself? I don't know about you, but I have a problem. I am ambitious; I am full of great ideas. I am also, however, extremely undisciplined. But the other day, I had an idea. What if I became "my manager"? Not a bad idea.

Contrary to what the multi-million dollar management training industry says, I don't think management is rocket science (though I am not saying it is easy). A good manager motivates and supports people and makes people accountable. To manage ourselves, we simply need to take concrete steps to motivate ourselves and make ourselves accountable.

1. Create a Personal Mission Statement

I think we get so caught up in the mundane details of daily life that we often lose track of why we're here, what we want, and, most importantly, what we value. Manage yourself by finding a way to integrate your values into what you do. Write your mission statement.

My mission statement, at the moment, is this: "To live simply and give selflessly, and to work diligently towards financial independence and the opportunities such independence will afford me."

Your mission statement doesn't have to be profound or poetic – it just needs to convey your core values and define why you do what you do each day. (Hint: If you can't find a mission statement that fits your current career or life, maybe it is time for a change!

2. Set Micro-Goals

There are countless benefits to writing down goals of all sizes. Annual, five-, and ten-year goals can help you expand on your mission statement because you know you are working towards a tangible result. But long-term goals are useless unless you have a strategy to achieve them. Manage yourself by setting micro-goals.

What is a micro-goal? I like to think of it as a single action that, when accomplished, serves as a building block to a much larger goal.

For example, the resolution to make a larger-than minimum monthly payment on a credit card balance is a micro goal. Each month you successfully increase your payment, you are closer to your big goal of getting out of debt.

At work, a micro-goal might involve setting up an important client meeting. Getting all the elements for a meeting in place is one step towards a larger goal of winning or increasing a particular business relationship.

A micro goal is not, however, anything that goes on your to-do list. Responding to a customer inquiry or cleaning out your cubicle is not a micro-goal unless, of course, you have bigger goals to specifically involving that customer or to get more organized.

Chapter 23:

<u>10 Habits of Cristiano Ronaldo</u>

Cristiano Ronaldo dos Santos Aveiro, famously known as Cristiano Ronaldo, was born on 5th February 1985 in Funchal, Madeira, Portugal. He is the last born in a family of four children. His father, José Dinis Aveiro, named the football legend after his favorite actor – Ronald Reagan.

Here are ten habits of Cristiano Ronaldo:

1.   <u>He pursues his dreams.</u>

Nothing stands in the way of Ronaldo and his dreams. In an interview with British reporters, his godfather – Fernao Sousa – recalls how young Ronaldo loved soccer. He could escape out of his bedroom window with a ball when he ought to be doing his homework. He could even skip meals to go play soccer.

Cristiano Ronaldo has played for great clubs like Manchester United, Real Madrid, Juventus and his national team – Portugal.

2.   <u>He knows how to package himself.</u>

Cristiano Ronaldo is one of the highly paid professional soccer players globally. Manchester United paid £12.24 million for young Ronaldo and he joined the club on 12th August 2003. It was a lot of money for a teenager but his expertise in soccer was unmatched.

On 11th June 2009, he left Manchester United for Real Madrid after the latter paid $131 million! His transfer from the London club was imminent but nobody expected such a high price could be paid for his services.

3. <u>He is hardworking.</u>

Ronaldo trains hard to play the best football game ever. His performance with Portugal against Manchester United amazed everybody and the club signed the young player after some of their players asked their manager to do so.

He told reporters that he was aware of the pressure to perform he would have at Real Madrid but he was up to the task. He confessed that he was ready for new challenges for him to become the best footballer.

4. <u>He knows how to handle victory.</u>

Cristiano Ronaldo has not let victory cloud his judgement. He has maintained his rationality despite being the world's most celebrated soccer player. He knows the responsibility on his shoulders of being a role model to many people globally.

He has bagged many awards in his football career including best Fifa Men's player (twice), ballon d'or (five times), UEFA best player in Europe (thrice), European champion, Champions league winner (five times) and many more. Cristiano Ronaldo has guarded himself from pride despite global recognition and all the accolades he has won.

5. He knows how to keep things private.

Ronaldo is a global football icon and his life is constantly under constant watch. It is almost impossible for him to live a private life. He is aware of this and has tried a lot to keep his personal life under wraps.

He has kept the status of his relationship to Georgina Rodriguez private with Italian media speculating that they had wed in Morocco. The couple has not come out to clear the air. The only information in the public is that they have a daughter together.

6. He loves parenting.

The football superstar loves parenting. He is not an absentee father. His relationship with his children is very good. He often trains his son – Cristiano junior – how to play soccer like him. A video of Ronaldo senior training with Ronaldo junior garnered 4 million views in 30 minutes on Instagram.

It is evident that the five times ballon d'or winner is doing a good job as a parent and coach because his son has scored 58 goals in only 28 games for the under-9s in Juventus.

7. He is responsible.

Cristiano Ronaldo is a responsible person. When he was still in Juventus, Massimiliano Allegri, tasked Ronaldo with the responsibility of inspiring the younger players in the team.

He confessed that Ronaldo is a great player and smart guy. He has never been the team captain at Juventus nor at Manchester United but he is a responsible team player and has been coordinating the team within and without the pitch.

8. He values family.

Ronaldo has demonstrated the importance of family. He had a close relationship with his father until the former succumbed to kidney related problems. He wanted his father to go to rehab to cure his alcoholism addiction but he declined his son's offer.

The football star has also taken care of his family by buying them a property worth £ 7 million in Portugal. He prioritizes the well-being of his family over anything in his life.

9. He is generous.

Cristiano is a generous man. He once sold a golden boot award in an auction that raised more than a million Euros. The proceeds were channeled towards building schools in Gaza. He similarly auctioned his award for best player of the year in 2017 and the funds were donated to the Make-A-Wish foundation.

He recently took a pay cut from March to June 2021 that cost him 3.8 million euros. He has also donated almost one million euros to hospitals in Portugal aid in the fight against the coronavirus pandemic.

10. He is patriotic.

Ronaldo is a patriotic citizen to his motherland, Portugal. He has lead the national soccer team to the world cup several times and also in European tournaments as the team captain. It is conspicuous that he has never been the team captain for any of the football clubs he has played for.

He accepted to pay a £ 16.6 million fine over tax evasion charges. He acted how a patriotic citizen would do instead of battling it in court to maneuver the charges against him.

In conclusion, these are the ten habits of the world's soccer G.O.A.T (greatest of all time).

Chapter 24:

<u>Happy People Use Their Character</u>
<u>Strengths</u>

One of the most popular exercises in the science of positive psychology (some argue it is the single most popular exercise) is referred to as "use your signature strengths in new ways." But what does this exercise mean? How do you make the most of it to benefit yourself and others?

On the surface, the exercise is self-explanatory:

a. Select one of your highest strengths – one of your **character strengths** that is core to who you are, is easy for you to use, and gives you energy;

b. Consider a new way to express the strength each day;

c. Express the strength in a new way each day for at least 1 week.

Studies repeatedly show that this exercise is connected with long-term benefits (e.g., 6 months) such as higher levels of happiness and lower levels of depression.

PUT THE EXERCISE INTO PRACTICE

In practice, however, people sometimes find it surprisingly challenging to come up with new ways to use one of their signature strengths. This is because we are very accustomed to using our strengths. We frequently use our strengths mindlessly without much awareness. For example, have you paid much attention to your use of self-regulation as you brush your teeth? Your level of prudence or kindness while driving? Your humility while at a team meeting?

For some strengths, it is easy to come up with examples. Want to apply **curiosity** in a new way? Below is a sample mapping of what you might do. Keep it simple. Make it complex. It's up to you!

- On Monday, take a new route home from work and explore your environment as you drive.
- On Tuesday, ask one of your co-workers a question you have not previously asked them.
- On Wednesday, try a new food for lunch – something that piques your curiosity to taste.
- On Thursday, call a family member and explore their feelings about a recent positive experience they had.
- On Friday, take the stairs instead of the elevator and explore the environment as you do.
- On Saturday, as you do one household chore (e.g., washing the dishes, vacuuming), pay attention to 3 novel features of the activity while you do it. Example: Notice the whirring sound of the vacuum, the accumulation of dust swirling around in the container, the warmth of the water as you wash the dishes, the sensation of the weight of a single plate or cup, and so on.

- On Sunday, ask yourself 2 questions you want to explore about yourself – reflect or journal your immediate responses.
- Next Monday….keep going!

WIDENING THE SCOPE

In some instances, you might feel challenged to come up with examples. Let me help. After you choose one of your signature strengths, consider the following 10 areas to help jolt new ideas within you and stretch your approach to the strength.

How might I express the character strength…

- At work
- In my closest relationship
- While I engage in a hobby
- When with my friends
- When with my parents or children
- When I am alone at home
- When I am on a team
- As the leader of a project or group
- While I am driving
- While I am eating

Chapter 25:

<u>10 Habits of Ed Sheeran</u>

<u>Background life of Ed Sheeran.</u>

Born on 17th February 1991 in Halifax in England, Edward Christopher Sheeran was born a musician. His passion for music was unmatched by any of his peers at early as when he was 4 years old. The 30-year-old Briton musician has come a long way and he has fans all over the globe who listen to his music.

Here are ten habits of Ed Sheeran:

1.   <u>He loves songwriting.</u>

Ed Sheeran started writing his self-composed songs even before he officially joined the industry. He has written over 30 songs which he has sung himself and another 45 that he has written for other artists.

This is evidence of his expertise in this field. It is impossible to be in music for the duration Ed Sheeran has been and not master one thing or another.

2.   <u>He is teachable and coachable.</u>

When Ed Sheeran was 11 years old, he was inspired by a backstage chat with Damien Rice. He asked Sheeran to write his music and he did exactly that.

In an exclusive interview, Ed Sheeran reveals that Damien inspired him in a way he only hopes to do for someone else. In his early years in music, he was under the tutelage of music giants and he earned collaborations with them.

3. He is hardworking.

In 2009 alone, Ed Sheeran performed in more than 300 live shows! He has always been writing songs tirelessly and releasing one album after another. He was only 14 years when he started recording CDs and selling them. After a while, he put all his songs together and released his first extended play (EP) titled The Orange Room.

While in his early teenage years, he wanted to perform in the city. He left home with his guitar and clothes for London where he wanted to expand his career.

4. He is social.

Ed Sheeran once shared that he does not use a phone. However, he maintains his interaction with his fans globally through social media. In 2010, he posted a video online that attracted Example's attention.

He invited him to a tour and Sheeran grew his online fan base exponentially. In the same year, he filled three new extended plays (Eps)!

5. He is consistent in doing music.

Not once has Ed Sheeran taken a break from doing music until the birth of his first daughter, Lyra on 1st September 2020. He took a hiatus from music to spend more time with family. Everything else comes second after his family.

Since the beginning of his career, Sheeran has consistently released hit music after another. His latest song currently is Shivers.

6. He is collaborative.

Sheeran has done many collaborations with other artists since he started his music career. In December 2017, he did a collaboration with Beyoncé in a song called *Perfect Duet*. Their song made it to number 1 on the billboard hot 100. Sheeran has also sung alongside Taylor Swift in a song called *Everything has changed*.

His other collaborations are with Justin Bieber in *I don't care*. He also featured The Weekend, Camila Cabello & Cardi B, and Eminem in *dark times, south of the border* and *river* respectively.

7. He is not shy.

Despite his private life, Sheeran is not shy as people may judge. The four-time Grammy award winner has made several appearances in films including *Bridget Jones's baby* in 2016 and *Yesterday* in 2019.

Sheeran has also acted in an episode in *Game of Thrones* and the Amazon anthology series, *Modern Love*.

8. He is brave.

With the growing fame, the winner of four Brit and four Ivor Novello awards has faced several lawsuits on copyright infringement. In 2014, two songwriters alleged that Ed Sheeran's photograph was taken from their track called *Amazing*.

Another copyright lawsuit against Sheeran in 2016 was dismissed by the courts in 2017. Other lawsuits followed in 2018 but were later settled. Ed Sheeran faced all of them, one after another.

9. He is patriotic.

Ed Sheeran was crowned with the Most Excellent Order of the British Empire on 7th December 2017 by Prince Charles.

He is recognized for his immense contribution to the music industry by his country because, despite his collaborations with other artists, he has maintained his patriotism to his country.

10. He is private.

He got engaged to his girlfriend Cherry Seaborn and they secretly got married. The only time Sheeran revealed this is when he was interviewed saying he is private with personal details.

In August 2020, the couple welcomed their first child daughter, Lyra Antarctica Seaborn Sheeran! It was the much that Ed Sheeran could say as he tried to keep his private life secretive.

In conclusion, these are the ten habits of Ed Sheeran, the renowned British award-winning songwriter, and artist.

Chapter 26:

<u>7 Habits That Are Good For You</u>

The cognitive ability to distinguish what is good from what is bad for us is an invaluable skill. Cherry-picking nutritive habits in a world full of all manner of indecency comes handy especially if you want to stand out from the crowd.

Here are 7 habits that are good for you:

1. <u>Waking Up Early</u>

The early bird catches the worm. Early risers have the opportunity to pick the best for themselves before the rest of the world is awake. It is healthy and prudent to wake up early and start your day before most people do. You leverage on opening your business early before your competitors. Besides, the preparedness of early risers is unmatched even as the day progresses.

Waking up early is not a reserve for 'busy people' only. It is for everyone in this world of survival for the fittest. We all have 24 hours in one day. The difference comes from how we use our time. One may spend more than 8 hours sleeping and another will spend just 6 hours for the same. You cannot sleep as if you are competing with the dead and expect to make it in the land of the living.

Early risers are active people. They are as alert as chamois, prepared for any eventuality.

2. Associate With Successful People

Show me your friends and I will show you what kind of person you are. Success, like most things, is contagious. In his book *48 laws of power*, Robert Greene writes *'avoid the unhappy and unlucky.'* This is not discrimination. Association with the unhappy and unlucky will contaminate you with negative energy.

Associate with successful people and you will follow their example. You will emulate their saving culture, their investment behavior, and their aggressiveness in business. In the shadow of the successful, you will attract positivity and grow exponentially. Maintain knit relationships with the successful.

3. Be Teachable

A teachable spirit will take you places where your character will not. A teachable person is capable of receiving correction graciously without perceiving it as demeaning. Do not be afraid of getting things wrong. Instead, be worried when you lack the humility to accept correction.

Being teachable is one of the greatest strengths you can have. We all are a work in progress, never finished products. What happens when you refuse to be under the tutelage of the successful and experienced? The greatest lessons are not learned in a classroom but the school of life.

4. Accepting Challenges

When challenged by circumstances we face, be the bigger brother/sister. Take challenges positively and work towards a solution instead of whining about this or that. Our patience, skills, and competence are sometimes put to the test. A test so subtle that we fail without even realizing it. When you have a positive mindset of accepting challenges, you will ace the game. Prove your worth wherever you are through your actions, never by your words.

When you accept a challenge and conquer it, it takes you to another level. The beauty of life lies in progress with the assurance that change is a constant. Accept challenges towards positivity and not the dark ones. Ignore that which derails your purpose or goes against your principles.

5. Learn When To Retreat and To Advance

The art of knowing when to push or pull is important in life. On the battlefield, retreating and advancing by troops is a call their leader makes. He decides that for his team based on his training, the immediate situation, and his judgment. Retreating is not a sign of weakness; neither is advancing a sign of strength. Both are strategies to win a war.

It is okay to retreat from a cause you were pursuing or to adjust your plans. Just make it worth your while. When you resume, be stronger than before. Again, when you retreat, do not succumb to the ridicule of your enemies when they mistake it for weakness. The fear of what the opinion of others (non-entities) is should not make you afraid of retreating to strategize.

When you make up your mind to advance with a noble course, advance skillfully. Do not advance blindly or ignorant of what you intend to achieve. Train your focus on the target.

6. Ask for help.

We are mortals; facing deficiencies here and there. We do not always have the answer to everything. Ask for help from the knowledgeable ones when in a quagmire.

Asking for help is not a weakness. It is appreciating the strengths of others. It is also appreciating the diversity of the human race that we are not endowed with everything. The silent rule is that you should be careful whom you approach for help. Some ill-intentioned people will sink you deep into trouble.

Nevertheless, asking for help is perfectly normal and it is something you should try sometimes. When you ask for help from the experienced, you save yourself the trouble of making messy mistakes. Learn through others who trod down the same road. Their lessons are invaluable; you will avoid their mistakes.

7. Develop hobbies.

Hobbies are those things you engage in for fun. They are very important because you take a break from your daily hustles. In your hobbies, you are carefree. You do not have to worry about your boss or business partners.

Hobbies are meant to be fun. If you are not having fun when doing your hobbies, probably they are no longer one. You should consider finding new ones. All work without play makes Jack a dull boy.

Hobbies are good for you. Go for swimming or that road trip, find a sport and play for fun, go beyond singing in the shower, travel everywhere you desire, or even start watching that TV series you are always curious about. Variety is the spice of life. Do not be afraid to spice up your life with all that your heart desires.

The above 7 habits are good for you. They will help you grow and increase your productivity in all you do.

Chapter 27:

<u>10 Habits of Shawn Mendes</u>

Shawn Peter Raul Mendes was born on 8th August 1998 in Toronto, Canada. The music superstar has rocked the industry with his talent which until 2013 was barely known.

These are ten habits of Shawn Mendes:

1. <u>He Is Social</u>

Shawn rose to fame in 2013 after posting his video cover of Justin Bieber's *as long as you love me* to his Vine social account. The six-second video spread like wildfire on the internet and netizens wanted to know more about the then 15-year-old teenager.

He currently has over 28 million YouTube subscribers and 64 million Instagram followers with whom he shares his life and work. He is outgoing and very interactive with his fans in his tours and live performances.

2. <u>He Is A Fast Learner</u>

Shawn Mendes is the embodiment of fast learning. His ability to comprehend and grasp skills faster than a majority of people is unmatched. Did you know that he learned how to play the guitar through YouTube?

In his interview with Spotify, he revealed that his father challenged him that he would get Shawn a guitar if he learned to play using a rented one for a couple of weeks. He accepted the challenge and started tutorials on YouTube.

3. He Is Hardworking

Shawn is a hardworking musician. Hitherto, he has released two live albums, four studio albums, twenty music videos, and three extended plays. All this has been accomplished within the short time he has been doing music.

Moreover, despite his rise to fame while still learning, Shawn has managed to juggle between music and academics successfully. He went for his world tour to further his music but still took online classes and managed to graduate with his class in 2016.

4. He Is Collaborative

Shawn is a rising superstar in music and he has featured other music giants in his songs. He has featured Camila Cabello on various tracks including *I know what you did last summer* and *Senorita* both of which have won several awards.

Other singers that have partnered with Shawn are Justin Bieber in *Monster*, Julia Michaels in *Like to be you*, and Khalid in *Youth*. He is open to more collaborations with other artists because he does not see them as a threat to his fan base.

5. <u>He Is Bold</u>

Shawn has been subject to many rumors since he came to the limelight. It was once rumored that he is gay and later also rumored that he had an affair with Taylor Swift and Camila Cabello. At all times, Shaw has maintained a straight face and such rumors have never made him shy away from music.

He once got a chance to clear the air when hosted by Dax Shepard in his podcast. He explained that he is not gay although he had close friends who were. It could be what contributed to the spreading of the rumors.

6. <u>He Is Ambitious</u>

Shawn is an ambitious young man pursuing his music career to the best he can make out of it. He has worked on several projects simultaneously as he completed his high school education. Nothing has obstructed his sight from pursuing his dreams.

He has done four world tours to promote his music and is looking forward to the wonder world tour from March 2022.

7. <u>He Is Visionary</u>

Shawn is a visionary young man. He has not forgotten his vision despite amassing wealth and fame. He launched the Shawn Mendes Foundation on 28th August 2019. This is a rare action by young celebrities worldwide. The foundation seeks to empower youth change makers, their organizations, and their work. As Shawn reminisces about his journey to starting music, he envisions an empowered society.

8. He Does Charity Work

Shawn has developed the habit of doing charity. Both through his foundation and other channels, Shawn has heavily given back to the community.

Some of the causes he has supported are disaster relief, education, abuse, grief support, homelessness, health, and senior citizen support.

9. He Loves Playing The Guitar

Shawn loves playing strings before he perfected his skill from YouTube video tutorials. From his teenage years, he has always moved with his guitar in every concert he performs.

He learned to play the guitar since he was 13 years and it has been his signature musical instrument despite him being able to hire instrumentalists.

10. He Is Creative

Shawn is a creative person. He has written hit songs one after another. This is growth from when he used to sing covers of other artists' songs. His creativity has expanded evident in how he connects with his fans through his songs.

In conclusion, these ten habits of Shawn Mendes are part of his lifestyle; some of which are hidden from the public.

Chapter 28:

<u>9 Habits To Wake Up Early</u>

Waking up early is a real struggle for many people. People are battling this friendly monster silently. Friendly because the temptation to snooze the alarm or turn it off completely when it rings in the morning is irresistible. Almost everyone can attest to cursing under their breath when they hear their alarm go off loudly in the morning.

Here are 9 habits that you should strive to incorporate into your life if you wish to make waking early a part of your routine:

1. <u>Sleeping early.</u>

It is simple – early to bed, early to rise. Retiring to bed early will give you enough time to exhaust your sleep. The average person ought to have at least 8 hours of sleep. Sleeping early will create more time for rest and enable you to wake up on time.

Since sleep is not ignorable, you may be embarrassed when you find yourself sleeping when attending a meeting, or when you are at work. Save yourself this shame by sleeping early to wake up earlier.

After a long day of vicissitudes, gift your body the pleasure of having a good night's rest. Create extra time for this by lying horizontally early enough.

2. <u>Scheduling your plans for the day beforehand.</u>

A good plan is a job half done. Before the day ends, plan for the activities of the next day. When it is all mapped out, you will sleep with a clear mind on what you will be facing the next day. Planning is not a managerial routine task alone but everyone's duty of preparing to fight the unknown the following day.

Waking up early is a difficult decision to make impromptu because of the weakness in yielding to the temptation of 'sleeping for only five more minutes.' Having a plan gives you a reason to wake up early.

3. <u>Creating deadlines.</u>

Working under pressure is an alternative motivation for waking up early if planning has failed. With assignments to submit within a short time, or work reports to be submitted on short notice, the need to wake up early to beat these deadlines will be automatic.

We can create deadlines and ultimatums for ourselves without waiting on our superiors to impose them on us. This self-drive will last longer and it will increase our productivity instead of waiting for our clients and employers to give us ultimatums.

4. <u>Being psychologically prepared.</u>

The mind is the powerhouse of the body. Mental preparedness is the first step towards making and sticking to landmark decisions. The mind should initiate and accept the idea of waking up early before you can comfortably adopt this new routine.

Develop a positive attitude towards rising early and all other subsequent results will fall in place. The first person you need to convince to move towards a particular cause is you. As simple as waking up early seems, many people are grappling with late coming.

This is fixable by making a conscious decision to turn around your sleeping habits. The greatest battle is fought in the mind, where the body antagonizes the spirit.

5. Finding like-minded friends.

Birds of the same feathers flock together. When you are in the company of friends with one routine, your habits are fortified. With no dissenting voice amongst your friends to discourage you from waking up early, your morning routine will find a permanent spot in your life.

The contrary is true. When you are the odd one out in a clique of friends who have no regard for time, you are likely to lose even the little time-consciousness you had. They will contaminate you with their habits and before you know it, you will slip back to your old self (an over sleeper).

When you also decide to be a loner and not associate with those with the same habits as yourself, then you risk giving up on the way. The psych from friends will be lacking and soon you will just revert to your old habits.

When you want to walk fast, walk alone. When you want to go far, walk with others.

6. Being sensitive to your environment.

It takes a man of understanding to read and understand the prevailing times and seasons. You may occasionally visit a friend or a relative and spend the night. How can you wake up way past sunrise in a foreign environment? This will suggest to your hosts that you are lazy.

Create a good image by waking up a little bit early. If allowed, help do some morning chores over there.

Adjust your routine accordingly. Win over people by waking up early to join them in their morning chores. It is there where friendships are forged. A simple habit of waking up early can be an avenue to make alliances.

7. Addressing any health issues early.

In case of any underlying health conditions that can stop you from waking up early in the morning, seek medical help fast. You may be willing to be an early riser but may be suffering from asthma triggered by the chilly weather in the morning.

When that condition is controlled, you can also manage to wake up a little bit earlier than before and engage in health-friendly activities in the morning. It is a win-win. In either case, going for a medical check-up frequently will keep you healthy to wake up early.

Your health is a priority and when taken care of you will wake up early.

8. It is a habit for the successful.

Ironically, those who have made it in life wake up earlier than the less established ones. One would think that it is the place of the less-founded ones to rise early to go to work and do business so that they can be at par with the wealthy and mighty. Instead, the reverse is true.

Follow the footsteps of great leaders who wake up early to attend to their affairs. They have become who they are because they give no room to the laziness of waking up late. We all have 24 hours in a day to do our businesses, where does the gap between the haves and the have-nots come from? That gap comes from how we use our time.

9. Having a cheerful Spirit.

A cheerful spirit finds joy in even what seems trivial. You should not see waking up early as punishment. It should be a routine to be followed happily religiously. When you have a cheerful spirit, knowing for whose benefit you rise early, then it will be a habit engraved into your spirit.

The above 9 habits to wake up early are key to discovering our purpose and build a new routine henceforth of being an early riser. The most successful people in the world abide by this routine so why not make it yours too.

Chapter 29:

6 Ways To Adopt New Actions That Will Be Beneficial To Your Life

There is this myth that goes around saying that, once you leave your teenage, you can never change your Habits. One can analyze this for themselves. Everyone has a list of new year's resolutions and goals. We hope to get these things done to some extent, but, never do we ever really have a clear idea of how to get to those goals in the least possible time.

We always desire a better future but never really know how to bring the necessary change in our lives. The change we need is a change in attitude and behavior towards life altogether. Change is never easy, but it is achievable with some sheer willpower. You might be on the right track to lead a better life, but there are always more and better things to add to your daily habits that can be helpful in your daily life.

Here are 6 simple yet achievable actions you need to take:

1. Decide Today What Is Most Important In Your Life

Life is a constant search for motivation. The motivation to keep doing and changing for the better. Once you have something to change for, take a moment and envision the rest of your life with and without the change you are about to make.

If you have made up your mind, now think about how you can start off with these things. For starters, if you want a healthy lifestyle, start your day with a healthy breakfast and morning exercise on an empty stomach. If you want to scale your business, make a customer-friendly business model.

2. Make Reasonable and Achievable Goals.

Adopting new habits can be challenging, especially if you have to change something in your day-to-day life to get better results. Start easy by making goals that are small, easy, reasonable, and won't give you a headache.

You can start off with baby steps. If you want to become more responsible, mature, and sorted in your life, just start your day by making your own bed, and do your dishes. Ride a bicycle to work, instead of a car or a bus. Things become smooth and easier once you have a reason for the hard acts.

3. Erase Distractions from Your Daily Life

You have wasted a lot already, don't waste any more time. As young as you are right now, you should feel more privileged than the older people around you. You have got the luxury of time over them. You have the right energy and pinnacle moments to seize every opportunity you can grasp.

Don't make your life a cluster of meaningless and profit-less distractions. You don't have to go to every public gathering that you are invited to. Only those that give you something in return. Something that you can avail yourself of in your years to come. Don't divulge in these distractions only for the sake of memories. Memories fade but the time you waste will always have its imprint in every moment that follows.

4. Make a Diary and a Music Playlist

You can devote some time to yourself, just to communicate with your brain and start a discussion with yourself. Most people keep a diary for this purpose, some people tend to make a digital one these days. When you start writing to yourself in the third person, talking and discussing your issues and your weaknesses, you tend to find the solutions within.

Most people find it comforting and calming when they have a playlist of music playing in the background while working. Everyone can try this to check if they get a better level of creativity if they have some small activity that soothes their stressed nerves.

5. Incorporate Regular Walk and Exercise in Your Life

When you know you have a whole day ahead of you, where you have to sit in an office chair for the next 8 hours. Where you have to sit in your home office looking at those sheets for most of the day. A 10 min walk before or after the busy schedule can help a lot in such conditions. You can never avoid physical activities for your whole life, especially if you want to live a healthier and longer life.

People always feel reluctant to exercise and running once they enter college or work life. Especially once they have a family to look out for. But trust me, your body needs that blood rushing once a day for some time. You will feel much more pumped and motivated after a hard 2-mile jog or a 15 min workout.

6. Ask Others for Help and Advice

You have a life to live for yourself, but always remember, you are never too old to ask for help. A human can never perfect something in their life. You will always find someone better than you at a particular task, don't shy to ask for help, and never hold back to ask for any advice.

We feel low many a time in our lives. Sometimes we get some foul thoughts, but we shouldn't ever pounce on them. We should rather seek someone's company for comfort and sharing our concerns.

Conclusion

The ultimate success in life is the comfort you get at the end of every day. Life can never be fruitful, beneficial, and worth living for if we don't arrange our lives as resourceful human beings. Productive minds always find a way to counter things and make the best out of everything, and this is the art of living your life.

Chapter 30:

6 Ways To Get Full Attention From People Around You

The long-term success of someone's life depends on getting the attention of others. Those others can include your teammates, your boss, your life partner, your clients, etc. But how? A person may ask. You cannot get promoted without getting your boss's attention, and your work cannot get appreciated by your teammates without awareness. To lead a healthy personal life, one may need to give attention to and from one's life partner, and of course, without the attention of your clients, how will your business survive?

Fortunately, there is plenty of research on how a human brain works and how it can focus on something. A lot of people have been researching about gaining people's attention for a long time now.

By some researchers, attention has been considered the "most important currency anybody can give you," although attention does make a person feel loved, it also gains your success. Fame can even come through negative attention, but it comes with hate as its price, whereas true and long-term success comes from positive attention. Here are six ways to get full attention from people around you.

1. Stand In A Central Position

When you are at a social gathering or a party, place yourself in a central position. Try to appear more friendly to new people, invite them over to your group, this way people will like you more. When you speak, they will pay attention—standing in a prominent place where everybody can see and talk to you easily will gain you more alert. Be being friendly to new individuals, and you will feel connected to others. Just be confident the whole time, and try to blend well with others and stand in a prominent place; this way, you will get more attention.

2. Leave Some Mystery!

Do you know what Zeigarnik Effect is? This effect suggests that the human brain tends to remember those things more, which is incomplete, as the question in their brain arises how? Where? And what?

This kind of technique is often used by professionals in business meetings, audience-oriented presentations. However, you can also use it in your daily life. When you introduce yourself to someone, don't just spill everything about yourself right away. Give the tiniest bit of pieces of information about something interesting, don't give the details just yet;

wait for someone to ask for the details. And someone will surely ask, and you will get the desired attention.

3. Use Body Language

Most of us know how to communicate verbally, but do you know how to communicate non-verbally? Because non-verbal communication is as important as verbal communication. Maintain positive body language, and if you sit back slouched and give some closed-off vibes, it is less likely that you would catch someone's attention. To see some attention, you need to bring more positivity in your conversation and your body language. Don't cross your arms and legs when talking to someone; face them with an open posture and stand with confidence. Don't avoid eye contact but don't overdo it; try to maintain eye contact with everyone around you for a while. This will show your confidence and also builds a connection with others. Be relaxed confidently. Smiling while talking to someone indicates your friendliness and makes them feel welcome; this way, they feel comfortable and give you their undivided attention, but everybody would avoid talking to you if you look moody.

4. Leave An Impression

It is the subconscious habit of a human being to think more about the people who left a good impression on them, try to engage their senses like touch, hear, or vision. Who doesn't like fashion nowadays? Try to wear something fashionable and decent, the kind of outfit that will likely leave a good impression on others. You can also wear something that has a different color or a twist to it. Speak confidently and in a clear voice. You can also put on a lovely perfume, cologne; try not to go overboard with this as nobody likes too much smell even if it is good.

5. Having A Hype Team

Having a hype team can easily capture a lot of attention; when you are in a not so formal setting, bring along your friends, surely they will be more than happy to excite you up. When you talk about your achievements among other people, it may seem to some that you are simply bragging. Still, when someone else talks about your accomplishments, it increases the interest of other people in you and gains you some positive attention.

6. Find A Way To Sell Yourself Without Bragging

A hype team is not always an option, but selling yourself without bragging is also something that needs to be done. What you don't need to discuss is;

- Your bank balance
- The expensive things you own
- Your occupation
- Your achievement

Conclusion

Brag through storytelling, and everybody loves an inspiring story. A successful person with a humble background always gains some attention. Attention plays an essential role in our lives, and you need to put a bit of effort into gaining it.

Chapter 31:

<u>5 Habits of Good Speech Delivery</u>

Speech delivery is a hot topic amongst many people with opinions divided on what to or what not to do. Everyone has their struggle in speech delivery; some are shy, others are bold but lack the material content to deliver while another group cannot hold a coherent conversation altogether with strangers.

Here are five fundamental habits of good speech delivery:

1. <u>Understand Your Audience</u>

Whenever given the chance to address an audience, it is imperative to understand the demographic constitution of your audience. Their age, social and political class contributes heavily to how they will perceive your speech.

The manner one can deliver a speech to a graduation class at a university is entirely different from how the same speech can be given to entrepreneurs considering the mindset and life priorities of these two groups.

When you have a thorough understanding of your audience, your art of public speaking and speech delivery will improve because your audience will relate well.

2. <u>Read The Mood and Setting of Your Audience</u>

The diction and language of your speech are variables of the prevailing mood of the audience. How can you relate with them if you are blind to their present mood (excitement or somberness) or the setting (high or low temperatures)?

The wearer of a shoe knows where it pinches. As a speaker, you should be flexible to allow your audience to follow your speech in their most comfortable state. If the weather is hot, allow them to open windows and air ventilation. If they are in a bad mood, make them understand that you feel their plight.

Be the bigger person in the room and accommodate everyone. It will earn you respect and your speech will be well received.

3. Understand the Theme of The Speech

This is the core subject matter of the speech. Every speech aims to pass a specific message to its recipients. Under no circumstances should the theme be lost to any other interest. If it does, the speech would be meaningless and a waste of time.

The onus is upon the deliverer of the speech to stick to the theme and neither alter nor dilute the message therein. He/she should first understand it to be able to convey the same to the audience. The speaker should not have any malice or prejudice to any section of the audience. They should have clean hands.

It is paramount to understand that the audience is not ignorant of the theme of the speech. When you disappoint their expectations, you would have lost their participation and some of them may leave the meeting in progress. The chance to deliver a speech does not render the rest of the audience is inferior to the speaker.

4. Be Bold

Boldness is the courage to speak fearlessly without mincing your words. Bold speakers are rare to come by and when they do, their audience becomes thrilled by their exuberance of knowledge. The content of a speech could be great but when a coward delivers it, the theme is lost. Boldness captures the attention of the audience. They expect the best from a bold speaker. The best orators of our time speak so powerfully that one cannot ignore them. The 44th president of the United States is a perfect example of how he boldly delivered his speeches and commanded respect across the globe.

A bold speaker does not bore his/her audience and they are more likely to remember a speech that they delivered compared to those of timid speakers. Fortune favors the bold.

5. Engage Your Audience

It is important to bring onboard your audience when you are delivering a speech. They will feel included and it will be more of a conversation than a talk down. When an audience actively participates in the delivery of a speech, it is more likely they will remember it.

As a speaker, maintain eye contact with the audience. This will create a connection with them and remove the notion that you are afraid of them. From time to time in your speech, rope them in to answer a relatable question. An audience expectant of engagement from its speaker will be more attentive.

A speech is not a monologue. It is an interaction between the speaker and his/her audience. When a speaker monopolizes a speech, it becomes boring and easily forgettable. It may further come out as a show-off rather than a genuine speech of a particular theme.

These are the five key habits if you want to maximize the delivery of your speech.

Chapter 32:

<u>Five Habits of Permanent Weight Loss</u>

Weight loss is a journey that many people have embarked on. Some of them are doing so out of personal ambition and others out of a doctor's advice. Regardless of their effort, somehow they seem not to be shedding off enough weight. Sometimes, even after losing a substantial amount of weight, they regain it once more and all their effort goes down the drain.

Here are five habits of permanent weight loss:

1. Win Both The Battle and The War

The mind is the arena of the greatest battle. Regardless that weight gain and loss manifests physically, the mind influences greatly on either outcome. When the battle is lost in the mind, the war against weight gain is subsequently lost.

Train your mind in a manner that suits you to be on the winning side. How so? A disciplined mind will win over your body to adhere to a strict routine geared towards weight loss. When you strengthen your mind not to succumb to temptations that will make you lapse in your weight loss journey, you have won half the battle.

As much as you put strategies in place to follow a particular routine, it is bound to fail if you have a weak mindset. No plan you put in place (that of weight loss included) will ever see the light of day when you are mentally unprepared. Similar to how one exercises body muscles, the brain too needs exercise. When your mind can withstand the temptations of eating anything, permanent weight loss is achievable.

2. Seek Professional Help

The best way to solve a problem is to involve experts. Their insight will diagnose the heart of the problem and prescribe a lasting solution. The journey of weight loss gets easier when you follow the advice of medical doctors. You will know what to do not to cause harm to your body.

The ambition of permanent weight loss may get in your way and make you try wild things to achieve your goal. Some people go to the extent of taking herbal concoctions with the belief that it will help them shed some weight. There are instances where these concoctions have caused more harm than the good they intended.

Most people ignore the advice of doctors regarding weight loss. Instead, they prefer some weird prescription of homemade beverages with the hope of permanent weight loss. There is no shortcut to reaching your goal. When you seek professional help regarding how to adjust your lifestyle, you will not lapse back or add extra weight. Permanent weight loss is achievable.

3. Associate With Like-Minded People

It is said that when you want to go fast, go alone but when you want to go far, go with someone. The journey of weight loss is long when you walk alone. Sometimes you may give up on the way and not achieve your goal.

In the company of people with whom you share a common goal – permanent weight loss –, you will encourage each other. In the small circle of friends, you will be able to exchange ideas and strategies for weight loss. This is unachievable when you isolate yourself.

The major challenge that may initially arise is finding the right group of people with whom you share a common goal. In the wrong group, you will be misplaced and permanent weight loss will forever remain a dream. Actualize this dream by excusing yourself from any rudderless group of people.

4. Lifestyle Change

A lifestyle change is a personal decision that one initiates without any external influence whatsoever. It is a conscious decision that one takes while being fully aware of the disruption it may have on his/her life.

Permanent weight loss is possible when one overhauls his/her lifestyle. When you stop taking alcohol or the habit of always driving even over short distances that you could walk, you will start shedding off some weight. Even an innocent habit of sleeping too much during the day will make you add some weight. Avoid it at all costs.

When you do a lifestyle audit and eliminate habits that will work against your goal of weight loss, the destination of permanent weight loss draws nearer. A lifestyle change is a difficult decision but one worth undertaking.

5. Seek Knowledge

Knowledge is power. Seek correct information on weight loss and avoid dwelling on myths, hearsay, and unfounded beliefs. Misinformation and misplacement of facts about weight loss will make it untenable. The fight against weight gain will have a big boost when there are sufficient facts about it.

The goal is not just weight loss but permanent weight loss. How is it achievable if we lack facts about it? Read and consult widely and approach it from a knowledgeable and informed point of view. Do not act blindly on fallacies.

These five habits for permanent weight loss bring significant change when adhered to.

Chapter 33:

Being Mentally Strong

Have you ever wondered why your performance in practice versus an actual test is like night and day? Or how you are able to perform so well in a mock situation but just crumble when it comes game time?

It all boils down to our mental strength.

The greatest players in sports all have one thing in common, incredibly strong beliefs in themselves that they can win no matter how difficult the circumstance. Where rivals that have the same playing ability may challenge them, they will always prevail because they know their self-worth and they never once doubt that they will lose even when facing immense external or internal pressure.

Most of us are used to facing pressure from external sources. Whether it be from people around us, online haters, or whoever they may be, that can take a toll on our ability to perform. But the greatest threat is not from those areas... it is from within. The voices in our head telling us that we are not going to win this match, that we are not going to well in this performance, that we should just give up because we are already losing by that much.

It is only when we can crush these voices that we can truly outperform our wildest abilities. Mental strength is something that we can all acquire. We just have to find a way to block out all the negativity and replace them with voices that are encouraging. to believe in ourselves that we can and will overcome any situation that life throws at us.

The next time you notice that doubts start creeping in, you need to snap yourself out of it as quickly as you can, 5 4 3 2 1. Focus on the next point, focus on the next game, focus on the next speech. Don't give yourself the time to think about what went wrong the last time. You are only as good as your present performance, not your past.

I believe that you will achieve wonderful things in life you are able to crush those negative thoughts and enhance your mental strength.

Chapter 34:

<u>10 Habits of Novak Djokovic</u>

The just-concluded French Open may probably have thrilled you, whether you are a tennis fan or not. With Novak Djokovic breaking more records and giving away his racket as a souvenir to a young boy. The Siberian Tennis Player is now ranked No. 1 in the world in men's singles. Djokovic's recent win isn't something new; he has been ranked no. 1 by ATP for over 300 weeks throughout his entire career. In 2016, he became the first player to hold all four Grand Slams simultaneously since Rod Laver, becoming one of the best players ever. Mesmerized by his tennis skills?

Here are 10 Novak Djokovic habits.

1. Envision Huge Dreams

According to Novak Djokovic says, embracing the process towards the world's best may belong, and tough, but it will pay you off. He used to watch Pete Sampras play and win, and it's when he started envisioning his win and made himself a trophy to that. When you believe in the possibility of achieving something, it becomes easier to learn skills for doing it.

2. Discipline and Dedication

Success is a consequence of many years of hard work and dedication. Your daily habits matter in everything. At only seven years, Novak had a burning desire to become the finest tennis player the world could ever have. Which later gave him the precision of what he needed to do. He devised a strategy for how much practice he would need to put in to become the best throughout his career.

3. Keep Improving

Limitations are merely mental constructs. Constant winning and growth require that you keep on enhancing your current skills. Because if you stop, others will catch up and surpass you. Novak is not the same as years ago; his desire to always top has led him to explore new things that potentially improve his game.

4. Master the Serve Return

Return serve proficiency is a vital shot in tennis. Novak is an excellent server; he has won more points on first and second return serves. Achieving such proficiency requires that you first make a body turn before moving your arm. This gives your body control and precision when returning the first serves. Moreover, you're able to take a bigger swing at the ball when your opponent's second serve seems average or weak.

5. Mental Struggles Is Part of the Sport

It can be so damaging to your confidence when you lose after dominating the tennis world for years. However, no one is immune. You have seen it with Tigger Woods in golf, and indeed, Novak has had his own to cope with. Pressure is part of tennis and a challenge to players. Accept and learn how to live with it.

6. Flexibility Is All It Takes

Flexibility is one of those aspects that, while vital in principle, is frequently overlooked in practice. For Tennis players, it is more on injury prevention than performance. Moreover, if you must maximize performance while preventing injury, how flexible you are saying it all. Novak has demonstrated flexibility as a weapon for maintaining balance and stability when tackling the game from extended positions.

7. Perseverance Is Key to Competitiveness

The route to the top is a rocky ride of ups and downs and mysterious impediments. It took Novak a journey of many continuous losses to reclaim his throne-which is a doubled challenge having been a dominant tennis player, but that's tennis. Tennis is very competitive, and the sooner you realize this, the better.

8. Better Late Than Never

Djokovic rose to prominence much later than his famous opponents, Federer and Nadal. When he won his first Grand Slam, they had already won many Grand Slams-though now he is at par with them. It also took time to be included in the list of the "big three." All you need is to act, work hard, and enjoy the game.

9. Don't Focus on Popularity

Surprisingly, and for a long time, Djokovic had no huge audience like his rivals, which could be noticed when he was up against them. Instead of letting this get to him, he turned it into motivation and fought extra hard. Let your accomplishments only raise your fan base.

10. Diet

Know your health issues, and stick to the diet your body needs. During the 2010 season, Novak experienced fatigue during matches. He lacked stamina and struggled with respiratory difficulties. He found out, with the help of a dietitian, that he was gluten and dairy intolerant.

Conclusion

Like Novak, whatever comes in your professional life is a product of discipline, dedication, and inspiration that comes from within you.

CPSIA information can be obtained
at www.ICGtesting.com
Printed in the USA
LVHW081959130122
708314LV00013B/568